The Student's Guide to

HISTORICAL THINKING

Going Beyond Dates, Places, and
Names to the Core of History

W0018126

LINDA ELDER, MEG GORZYCKI, and RICHARD PAUL

ROWMAN & LITTLEFIELD
Lanham · Boulder · New York · London

Originally published by
The Foundation for Critical Thinking
1-800-833-3645
www.criticalthinking.org

Reissued in 2019 by Rowman & Littlefield
An imprint of The Rowman & Littlefield Publishing Group, Inc.
4501 Forbes Boulevard, Suite 200, Lanham, Maryland 20706
www.rowman.com

6 Tinworth Street, London SE11 5AL, United Kingdom

Copyright © 2011 by Linda Elder

All rights reserved. No part of this book may be reproduced in any form or by any electronic or mechanical means, including information storage and retrieval systems, without written permission from the publisher, except by a reviewer who may quote passages in a review.

British Library Cataloguing in Publication Information Available

Library of Congress Cataloging-in-Publication Data Is Available

ISBN 978-0-944583-46-3 (pbk)
ISBN 978-1-5381-3394-1 (electronic)

The Foundation for Critical Thinking and the Thinker's Guide Library

Founded by Dr. Richard Paul, the Foundation for Critical Thinking is the longest-running non-profit organization dedicated to critical thinking. Through seminars and conferences, online courses and resources, and a wide range of publications, the Foundation promotes critical societies by cultivating essential intellectual abilities and virtues in every field of study and professional area. Learn more at www.criticalthinking.org and visit the Center for Critical Thinking Community Online (criticalthinkingcommunity.org).

The Thinker's Guide Library introduces the Paul-Elder Framework for Critical Thinking™ and contextualizes critical thinking across subject areas and audience levels to foster fairminded critical reasoning throughout the world.

1. The Miniature Guide to Critical Thinking Concepts & Tools, Eighth Edition
2. The Thinker's Guide to Analytic Thinking
3. The Thinker's Guide to Ethical Reasoning
4. The Thinker's Guide to Socratic Questioning
5. The Thinker's Guide to Fallacies
6. The Nature and Functions of Critical & Creative Thinking
7. The Art of Asking Essential Questions, Fifth Edition
8. The Thinker's Guide to the Human Mind
9. The Thinker's Guide for Conscientious Citizens on How to Detect Media Bias and Propaganda in National and World News, Fourth Edition
10. The Thinker's Guide to Scientific Thinking
11. The Thinker's Guide to Engineering Reasoning
12. The Thinker's Guide to Clinical Reasoning
13. The Aspiring Thinker's Guide to Critical Thinking
14. The Student Guide to Historical Thinking
15. The Thinker's Guide for Students on How to Study & Learn a Discipline, Second Edition
16. How to Read a Paragraph: The Art of Close Reading, Second Edition
17. How to Write a Paragraph: The Art of Substantive Writing
18. The International Critical Thinking Reading and Writing Test, Second Edition
19. The Miniature Guide to Practical Ways for Promoting Active and Cooperative Learning, Third Edition
20. How to Improve Student Learning: 30 Practical Ideas
21. A Critical Thinker's Guide to Educational Fads
22. The Thinker's Guide to Intellectual Standards
23. A Guide for Educators to Critical Thinking Competency Standards

Contents

Introduction

Everyone thinks about the past, but few people think critically about how they have come to think about the past. Most of us do not recognize that the stories we tell ourselves about the past are examples of historical thinking. What is more, these stories are often riddled with distortions of our own making. Our view of the past is largely prejudiced by the ideologies of the cultures and groups that have influenced us. We see the past through the lenses we have created in our own minds. We want to see the past in a certain way, so we do. We have been taught to see the past in a certain way, so we see it that way. We rarely question the cultural norms, customs, beliefs, taboos, and values that influence our conceptualizations of history.

If we are to create fairminded critical societies, societies in which all peoples, nations and cultures come to value fairminded critical thinking, we will need to think critically about history. We will need to see the past in ways that are less biased. We will need to use our understanding of the past to help us make better decisions in the present and future.

The purpose of this guide is to help you begin to understand history as a way of thinking, as a system of understandings. History is not a list of dates, names, and events to store up in your memory. It is a catalog of stories told about the past that, when told and understood insightfully and deeply, can help us live better in the future.

Every historical account has been told from some perspective, and that perspective can be analyzed and assessed using the tools of critical thinking. In fact, if you don't analyze and assess historical thought using these tools, you will likely uncritically accept views about the past that are distorted, illogical, based in biases or prejudices, or just plain nonsense. We believe that the concepts and principles of critical thinking introduced in this guide are essential to any serious study of history. All the best historians use these tools, though perhaps not explicitly. When you master critical thinking as it applies to history, you learn history. At the same time, you can learn the tools of critical thinking as you study history. But you cannot effectively study history without these tools.

In this guide, we begin with some essential understandings about the relationship between history and thinking and about the concept of historical thinking itself. In Part Two we offer suggestions for how to become a master student in history. In Part Three we introduce the basic concepts of critical thinking and how they apply to the study of history. In Part Four we briefly discuss some problems and issues in historical thinking.

This is not a guide to be read once; rather, it should be read and applied and read and applied, again and again. The principles that underlie it lend themselves to application at deeper and deeper levels.

Part One: Learning to Think Historically

How to Study and Learn History

The Problem:

Students are required to take a number of history classes while in school, but few come to see history as a mode of thinking or system of interconnected ideas. History is still generally taught as a series of names, dates, and places. Instruction in history sometimes helps students learn to detect a degree of cause and effect. But students are not typically taught to think critically while reading historical accounts, or to write critically when composing essays on historical events, issues and ideas. Students, for the most part, are not taught to listen critically during discussions on history. They are not taught to think through historical concepts, nor internalize foundational historical meanings. They are not usually encouraged to make connections between history and important events in life.

Even the best students are often unable to make connections between the past and the present because they have not learned to think critically about evidence or lack of evidence, the historian's perspective, or the implications of a particular narrative.

How do you see history? To what extent do you think you have been taught to see history as a system of understandings which, when understood deeply, can help you live better? Or, conversely, to what extent have you come to see history as a disconnected list of names and events and places and times?

Some Basic Definitions:

Critical thinking is the kind of thinking—about any subject, content, or domain—that improves itself through disciplined analysis and assessment. Analysis requires knowledge of the elements of thought; assessment requires intellectual standards for thought. *Historical thinking* is, among other things, thinking about the past in order to live better in the present and the future. There are two forms of historical thought. One entails merely thinking about the past. Everyone is a historical thinker in this sense. The other entails thinking critically about the past. This means using the concepts and principles of critical thinking to create understandings of the past.

The Solution:

To study history well, and learn to think critically about history, is to learn how to think in a disciplined way about history. It is to learn to think within the logic of history, to:

- raise vital historical questions and problems, formulating them clearly and precisely;

- gather and assess historical information, using historical ideas to interpret that information insightfully;

- come to well-reasoned historical conclusions and interpretations, checking them against relevant criteria and standards;

- adopt the point of view of the skilled historian, recognizing and assessing, as need be, historical assumptions, implications, and practical consequences;

- communicate effectively with others using the language of history and the language of educated public discourse; and

- relate what one is learning in history to other subjects and to what is significant in human life.

To become a skilled historical thinker is to become a self-directed, self-disciplined, self-monitored, and self-corrective historical thinker, who assents to rigorous standards of thought and mindful command of their use.

Essential Idea: The skills of critical thinking are necessary for learning to think historically.

Understanding History as Historical Thinking

History, Like All Subjects, Represents A Systematic Way of Thinking.

A key insight necessary for deep learning of history is that history should be understood as an organized, integrated way of thinking.

Organized Systematically by Ideas.

Learning history entails learning the ideas that historians use to define and structure history. Learning a historical concept entails learning how to use it in thinking through some historical question or issue. Hence, to understand the idea of *power* in history is to learn how people have used power to get what they want. To understand the idea of *exploitation* in history is to learn how people with power have used people with little or no power to get what they want. To understand how and why people in power have exploited those with little or no power is to understand the role of *irrationality* in the pursuit of power. It is to understand, in other words, that people are often selfish and therefore unwilling to consider how their misuse of power (to get something for themselves) might harm others. It also entails understanding that people are often willing to deny the rights and needs of those outside their group to get something for their group – money, power, prestige, and so forth. In sum, the concepts of *power*, *exploitation,* and *irrationality* are concepts that historians often use to understand why and how people have behaved in certain ways throughout history. These are just some of the many concepts historians use to reason through historical problems and issues.

Leading to a Systematic Way of Questioning.

Ideas within history are intimately connected with the kinds of questions historians ask. In other words, history represents ways of asking and answering a body of questions. There is no way to learn historical content without learning how to figure out reasonable answers to historical questions and problems. For instance, historians might ask: What variables contributed to the development of these circumstances at this period in history, which led to these consequences? What patterns in human behavior can be identified by studying history? How can understanding these patterns help us live better in the present and in the future? (For more key questions historians ask, see The Logic of History, pages 36-39.)

Essential Idea: History, like all subjects, represents an integrated way of thinking, defined by a system of ideas, leading to a distinctive and systematic way of questioning.

Approaching History Classes
as Historical Thinking

When you understand history as a way of thinking, you approach the study of history very differently from the typical student. Consider how a student who understands history as historical thinking might approach a history course:

"To do well in this course, I must begin to think historically. I must not read the textbook as a bunch of disconnected stuff to remember but as the thinking of the historian who wrote it. I must begin to be clear about historical purposes. (What are historians trying to accomplish?) I must begin to ask historical questions (and recognize the historical questions being asked in the lectures and textbook). I must begin to sift through historical information, drawing some historical conclusions. I must begin to question where historical information comes from. I must notice the historical interpretations that the historian forms to give meaning to historical information. I must question those interpretations (at least sufficiently to understand them). I must begin to question the implications of various historical interpretations and begin to see how historians reason to their conclusions. I must begin to look at the world as historians do, to develop a historical viewpoint. I will read each chapter in the textbook looking explicitly for the elements of thought in that chapter. I will actively ask (historical) questions in class from the critical thinking perspective. I will begin to pay attention to my own historical thinking in my everyday life. I will try, in short, to make historical thinking a more explicit and prominent part of my thinking."

When you approach history classes as historical thinking, you begin to understand the historical dimension of other subjects as well. For example, you begin to recognize that every subject itself has a history and that the present state of the subject is a product of its historical evolution. You also notice the overlap between history as a study of the relatively recent past of humans (the last 30,000 years) and the much longer history of humans (canvassed in anthropology). You are able to place these last 30,000 years (which seem a long time when we first think of it) into the larger historical perspective of anthropology. This perspective begins its study of the human past some 2,000,000 years ago when our ancestors were small, hairy, apelike creatures who used tools such as digging sticks and clubs, walked upright and carried their tools. You are able to see humans moving from hunting and gathering civilizations, to agricultural civilizations, to industrial civilizations, to post-industrial civilizations, to the age of information.

When you think historically, you are able to take a historical perspective and put it into a larger historical view by shifting from anthropological thinking to geographical thinking. You understand that human history is itself a small part of a much older history, that of mammals, and that the age of mammals was preceded by an age of reptiles, and that by the age of coal-plants, and that by the age of fish, and that by the age of mollusks. You can then take the next step and grasp that geological history, even though reaching back thousands of millions of years, is comparatively short when compared to that of the solar system, while that of the solar system is comparatively short when compared to that of the galaxy.

Your capacity to think historically in larger and larger time spans continues to develop as your study of all subjects is transformed by a developing sense of the drama of time itself. You are then able to shift from history to pre-history, from pre-history to anthropological history, from anthropological history to geological history, and from geological history to astronomical history. In this ever-expanding perspective, the history of human knowledge is pitifully short: a milli-second geologically, a microsecond astronomically. It is only a second ago—astronomically speaking—that a species has emerged, *Homo sapiens*, which drives itself, and creates the conditions to which it itself must then adapt in new and unpredictable ways. It is only a milli-second ago that we have developed the raw capacity, though not the active propensity, to
think critically.

Essential Idea: When you approach history classes as historical thinking, you see applications of history to related subjects. Doing so increases the power of historical thinking and learning.

Understanding and Taking Command of Your Personal History

In a broad sense, you are a historical thinker. You tell yourself stories about the past, as do all humans. Your life can be thought of as "chapters" you have written in your mind (your "book"). You create memories of "your past." You "write" or create them as they are happening and you often "rewrite" or recreate them over time.

Much of the story you are creating, much of your "personal history," has been colored by wishful thinking, by the way you would like to see yourself. Much of your "history" is shaped by the people who have influenced you throughout your life—your parents, teachers, siblings, and friends. It is shaped by the people who are influencing you now. If you were to write an autobiography, it would not be an objective detailing of things that happened to you and things you have done; it would be a mixture of fact and distortion—of things that actually did happen and things *that just seem (in your mind) to have happened.*

In taking command of your personal history, strive to achieve an objective view of the conditions and factors that have contributed to your way of seeing the world and your place in it. While it may not be possible to achieve a completely objective perspective, it is possible for you to increase your awareness and understanding of certain assumptions that might be problematic. Some questions that might be useful in the process of constructing your own history include:

- Who are my parents or guardians, and what were their lives like before I was born?

- What were the dominant beliefs, concerns, values, and assumptions that influenced the way my parents or guardians raised me?

- What dominant ideas was I expected to accept uncritically in my schooling and through religious teachings?

- Who were the people that influenced me the most? How did they influence me?

- When did I begin to have a sense of myself as an individual with unique ways of seeing and doing things? What did that experience mean to me then? How does that way of seeing influence my thinking now?

- What do I remember as the most significant events in my life, and why are they significant?

- What do others remember about me, and the events that impacted me? How are the memories, perspectives, and conclusions of others about me different from my own? What can the memories, perspectives, and conclusions of others teach me about my life?

• What assumptions do I have about who I am, what I am able to do with my life, what I am obligated to do with my life, and what my life means? Am I open to changing these assumptions? Are there reasons why it might be advantageous to change these assumptions?

You can be the master of your personal history. You can decide whether to write the story of your life in ways that mirror or distort reality. You can decide whether to write the story of your past in largely negative or positive terms. In writing your story, you can highlight the positives and give less attention to the negatives, or you can highlight the negatives and downplay the positives. You can write your story insightfully or in a prescribed way. You can look beneath the surface of events and happenings for deeper meanings, or you can think in a limited, provincial way about them.

Either way, you are a historical thinker—not necessarily a good historical thinker, but a historical thinker nonetheless.

Realize that historical thinking can have at least two different meanings:

1. Any type of thinking about the past,
2. Thinking about the past in ways that are logical, reasonable, and which mirror what actually happened in the past.

Historians attempt to do the second, think about the past in ways that make most sense, in ways that are accurate or the most logical in context. Of course, historians don't always succeed at this because they are fallible—they make mistakes. Some are better than others at thinking critically about history.

Because you think about your past, it makes sense for you to think like a skilled historian about your past, to think critically about your past. You want to think critically about both the past that is behind you and the past that is being created every day. The way you think about your life is a product, not only of what happens to you, but how you see it. You have no control over what actually has happened to you to this point. But you do control how you see it. And, most importantly, you can significantly influence what happens in the present and in the future.

You will, and do, tell the story of your life, in your mind, at every phase of your life. There is, in other words, an ongoing narrative you create which is, in your mind, the story of your life (to that point). Are you trapped in that story or emancipated by it? Are you defining how you see your past? Are you shaping what you do today? Are you in control of your future? All of these questions are intimately connected with history, your personal history. And for you, there is perhaps no more important history.

Essential Idea: You can take command of your personal history. You can determine how you see your past and the actions you take in the future. Or you can let other people or groups define how you see your personal history.

Part Two:
Becoming a Proficient Student of History

Thinking Within Historical Ideas

Learning to think within the ideas of a subject is like learning to perform well in basketball, ballet, or on the piano. Thinking within the ideas of a subject at an advanced level without disciplined practice is as unnatural to the human mind as sitting down at a piano and spontaneously playing Chopin's "Polonaise."

Merely sitting through lectures on history will not teach you how to think historically. You must therefore set out to discover how to think like a historian. You will not discover this thinking by cramming into your head large masses of partially digested contents of a history textbook or sets of lectures. Here is what we recommend.

Recognize that you are seeking a new way to look at learning history. Recognize that it will take time to become comfortable in this new perspective. Consider your task as a student to be learning new ways to think. Stretching the mind to accommodate new ideas is crucial.

Recognize that there are key ideas behind history that give it a unified meaning. Look up a variety of definitions or other conceptualizations of history (use dictionaries, textbooks, encyclopedias). Remember that you are looking for the ideas that give a unified meaning to history and thus enable you to experience it as a system. Try to find the common denominator of history as a field of study. Ask your instructor for help.

Now relate every new historical idea (in the textbook or lectures) to the fundamental idea with which you began. The big idea with which you began should be in the background of all new ideas. Seek intuitive connections—connections that make complete sense to you.

Essential Idea: There are basic ideas that act as guide-posts to all thinking within a subject. Look for these basic ideas in studying history and stretch your mind to learn them. Weave everything else into them.

Raising Important Historical Questions

Every discipline is best known by the questions it generates and the way it goes about settling those questions. To think well within history, you must be able to raise and answer important questions in it. At the beginning of a semester of historical study, try generating a list of at least 15 questions that history seeks to answer. To do this, you might read an introductory chapter from the textbook or an article on the discipline. Then explain the significance of the questions to another person.

As your courses proceed, add new questions to the list, underlining those questions when you are confident you can explain how to go about answering them. Regularly translate chapter and section titles from your history textbooks into questions. For example, a section on the American Civil War may attempt to answer the question: What were the primary causes and implications of the Civil War? A section on "cause and effect" may attempt to answer these questions: How does it make best sense to conceptualize cause and effect in history? What are some different ways historians think of cause and effect?

In addition, look for key historical questions in every lecture. Relate basic historical questions to the differing theories historians use to think through historical issues. Master fundamental questions well. Do not move on until you understand them.

Notice interrelationships between key ideas and key questions. Without the ideas, the questions are meaningless. Without the questions, the ideas are inert—there is nothing you can do with them. A skilled historical thinker is able to take historical questions apart, generate alternative meanings, distinguish leading from subordinate questions, and grasp the demands that historical questions put upon the historical thinker.

Essential Idea: If you want to learn the essential content of history you must become skilled at asking historical questions.

Asking Questions About History as a Field of Study

Answer as many of these questions as you can by examining historical texts. You may need help from your instructor on some of them.

1. To what extent are there competing schools of thought within history?

2. To what extent do experts in history disagree about the answers they give to important questions?

3. What other fields deal with some of the same content historians deal with but perhaps from a different standpoint? To what extent are there conflicting views about this content in light of these different standpoints?

4. To what extent, if at all, is history properly called a science?

5. To what extent can historical questions be answered definitively? To what extent are historical questions matters of (arguable) judgment?

6. What are some of the various methods historians use to verify their claims and justify their conclusions of past events?

7. To what extent is there public pressure on historians to compromise their professional practice because of public prejudice or vested interest?

8. What does the history of history as a discipline tell you about the status of knowledge in the field? How old is the field? How common is controversy over fundamental terms, theories, and orientation?

Essential Idea: Many disciplines are not definitive in their pursuit of knowledge. As you study history, it is important to understand the extent to which it deals with definitive knowledge.

Asking Questions About History Books

All history books, as indeed all books, are products of reasoning. Hence, they can be analyzed using the elements of reasoning, and assessed by applying intellectual standards to these elements. In addition, you can ask the following questions about your history books. To answer them, you may need some help from your instructor.

1. Since there are competing schools of thought within history, what is the orientation of the writer(s)? Do these writers highlight competing schools within history and detail the implications of that debate?

2. Are other books available that approach history from a significantly different standpoint? If so, to what extent might this book be biased?

3. Would history experts disagree with any of the answers given in this book to important questions? How would they disagree?

4. Are there books in other fields that deal with the same content in this book (from a different standpoint, perhaps)? To what extent are there conflicting views about this subject in light of these different standpoints?

5. To what extent does this book represent history as a science? If so, do some history experts in the field disagree with this representation?

6. To what extent do the historical questions asked in this book lead to definitive answers? Conversely, to what extent are questions in this book matters of (arguable) judgment? And does the book help you distinguish between these very different types of questions?

Essential Idea: Not all history books are equal as to quality. As you read a history book, it is important to distinguish its strengths from its limitations.

Problems with History Textbooks

Democracy can be an effective form of government only to the extent that the public (that rules it in theory) is well informed about national and international events and can think independently and critically about those events. Hence, people cannot have a true democracy when their understanding of history comes from textbooks filled with bias and propaganda. Yet this tends to be the case the world over.

If students don't learn to recognize bias in their nation's textbooks, if they can't recognize propaganda when exposed to it in textbooks, if they cannot detect ideology, slant and spin in their textbooks, they cannot reasonably determine what parts of a textbook should be supplemented, counter-balanced or thrown out entirely.

Textbooks can be effective instruments of learning only to the extent that you, the student reader, learn to read them critically. Most students and teachers assume that their country's textbooks are more objective and more fairly written than those of any other nation. Educated persons come to reject this uncritical belief as they discover how textbooks are written and chosen.

Textbooks are primarily published to make money, not to enlighten students or the public. Textbooks yield high profits when chosen by large districts. And textbooks are fundamentally chosen in accordance with the mainstream views of a given culture. In other words, teachers and school administrators tend to choose textbooks whose authors present "history" in terms of what people in the culture already believe or want to believe. History teachers, frequently entrenched in the ideologies of the culture, unconsciously expect their textbooks to entail their culture's belief systems, just as people in the culture unconsciously expect the daily "news" to fit the same belief systems.

In his book, *Lies My Teacher Told Me*, sociologist James Loewen[1] catalogues a number of problems with history textbooks. These problems came to light for Loewen as he studied commonly used history textbooks over a number of years. Loewen says history textbooks in the U.S. fail to present a reasonable view of our past—glorifying our country, distorting the truth, and grossly misleading students. Referring to American history textbooks, he says:

> *The stories that history textbooks tell are predictable; every problem has already been solved or is about to be solved. Textbooks exclude conflict... They leave out anything that might reflect badly upon our national character. When they try for drama, they achieve only melodrama, because readers know that everything will turn out fine in the end.[2]*

History should be taught so that you, the student, come to see a deep connection between how your life today has been influenced by the past, by how you perceive the past, by how past events have been presented to you by your culture. But history textbooks tend to take a simplistic view of history. As Loewen puts it "...textbooks seldom use the past to illuminate the present. They portray the past as a simpleminded morality play. 'Be a good citizen' is the message that textbooks extract from the past. 'You have a proud heritage. Be all that you can be.' "[3]

There are a number of reasons why history textbooks fail to live up to their promise– including nationalism, which is a form of group think, or sociocentric thought. Loewen says "Textbooks are often muddled by the conflicting desires to promote inquiry and to indoctrinate blind patriotism … The titles themselves tell the story: *The Great Republic, The American Pageant, Land of Promise, Triumph of the American Nation …* And you can tell history textbooks just from their covers, graced as they are with American flags, bald eagles, the Washington Monument."[4]

Loewen believes that history textbooks conceal the true nature of history. He says:

> *History is furious debate informed by evidence and reason. Textbooks encourage students to believe that history is facts to be learned. "We have not avoided controversial issues," announces one set of textbook authors; "instead, we have tried to offer reasoned judgments" on them – thus removing the controversy! Because textbooks employ such a godlike tone, it never occurs to most students to question them.*[5]

As a student of history, you have probably been taught to uncritically accept what is in your history textbooks. One student of Loewen's regrets this blind acceptance: "In retrospect I ask myself, why didn't I think to ask, for example, who were the original inhabitants of the Americas, what was their life like, and how did it change when Columbus arrived? … However … everything was presented as if it were the full picture so I never thought to doubt that it was."[6]

If you are using a history textbook for a given course, compare it with other history textbooks for the same course; identify where there is overlap and where there might be disagreement among the authors (one of Loewen's suggestions). Then locate some alternative ways of looking at a given historical time period or a given set of historical events (found in history books or, preferably, original sources) and see how the textbook deals with the same time period or set of events. See if you can detect propaganda and bias in the textbook. See if you can recognize when your country is being glorified at the expense of the truth. You might need help with this one, but we suggest that you begin by looking at a couple of typical history textbooks and then compare what is found in them with what is found, for instance in Loewen's book referenced here, or in Howard Zinn's, *A People's History of the United States.*[7]

Understanding the Role of Questions in Historical Thinking and Learning

Historical thinking is not driven by historical answers but by historical questions. Had no historical questions ever been asked by scholars, history as a field of study would never have developed in the first place. Furthermore, history stays alive as a field of study only to the extent that fresh questions are generated and taken seriously as the driving force in thinking. To think through or rethink any issue in history, one must ask questions that stimulate historical thought. Historical questions define historical tasks, express historical problems and delineate historical issues. Answers, on the other hand, often signal a full stop in historical thought. Only when an answer generates a further question does thought continue. This is why it is only when you are asking historical questions that you are really thinking through and learning history.

So, instead of trying to store a lot of disconnected facts and names and places in your mind, start asking historical questions. Deep historical questions drive thought beneath the surface of things, forcing you to deal with complexity. Questions of purpose force you to define tasks. Questions of information force you to look at sources of information as well as assess the quality of information. Questions of interpretation force you to examine how you are organizing or giving meaning to information. Questions of assumption force you to examine what you are taking for granted. Questions of implication force you to follow out where your thinking is leading you. Questions of point of view force you to examine your perspective and to consider other relevant viewpoints.

Questions of relevance force you to discriminate what does and what does not bear upon a question. Questions of accuracy force you to evaluate and test for truth and correctness. Questions of precision force you to give details and be specific. Questions of consistency force you to examine your thinking for contradictions. Questions of logic force you to consider how you are putting the whole of your historical thought together, to make sure that it all adds up and makes sense within a reasonable system of some kind.

Continually remind yourself that significant learning in history begins when deep and important historical questions are asked.

Essential Idea: If you want to learn history, you must ask questions that lead to further questions that lead to further questions. To learn history well is to learn to ask deep and important historical questions.

Distinguishing Two Kinds of Historical Questions

In approaching a historical question, it is helpful to determine the kind of system to which it belongs. Is it a question with one definitive answer? Alternatively, does the question require us to consider competing answers or even competing ways of conceptualizing the question?

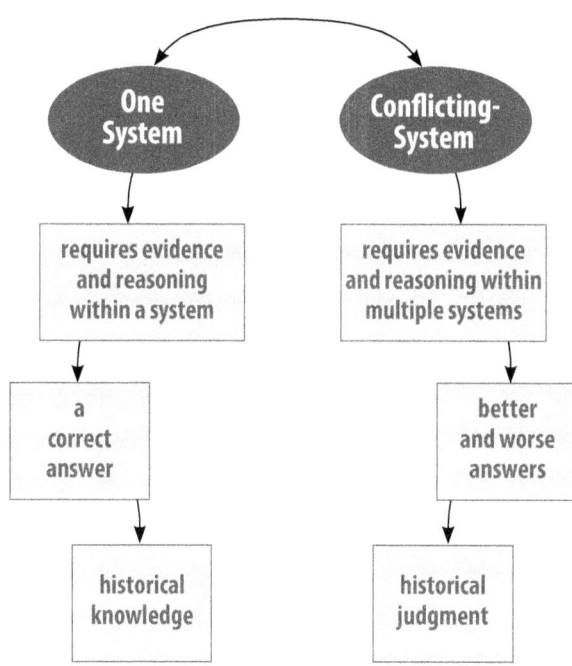

Questions of Procedure or Fact (one system or established system; the thinker is required to find the correct system)—These include questions with an established procedure or method for finding the answer. These questions are settled by facts, by definition, or both. They are prominent in mathematics as well as the physical and biological sciences. But they are used in historical thinking wherever facts are relevant and can be obtained. Examples include:

- What constitutional amendment made slavery in the U.S. illegal?
- From what countries were slaves taken, for use in the U.S., prior to the Emancipation Declaration?
- At what age were girls allowed to marry in 1940 in Massachusetts?

- At what age are girls legally allowed to consent to sex in Italy today?
- What is the legal definition of statutory rape in the U.S.? Has this definition changed over time?
- What technical achievements made trans-oceanic travel possible in the 15th century?
- Who were the Romanov monarchs?
- On what date did Abraham Lincoln deliver what is now known as the Gettysburg Address?
- On what date did Neal Armstrong first set foot on the moon?
- How many American soldiers died at the Bay of Pigs?
- Of all the major military engagements the United States has been involved in, which war claimed the greatest number of American lives?
- Who is considered the primary author of the American Declaration of Independence?
- Of the four Civil War battles listed, which claimed the greatest number of total lives: Gettysburg, Shiloh, Antietam, Chickamauga?

Questions of Judgment (multi-systems or conflicting systems, within which the reasoner is required to think)—Questions requiring reasoning, but with more than one arguable answer. These are questions that make sense to debate, questions with better-or-worse answers (well-supported and reasoned or poorly-supported and/or poorly-reasoned). Here we are seeking the best answer within a range of possibilities. We evaluate answers to such questions using universal intellectual standards such as breadth, depth, logicalness, and so forth. Some of the most important historical questions are conflicting-system questions (for example, those questions with an ethical dimension). Examples of questions of judgment include:

- What variables were most responsible for the French Revolution?
- What was the most significant consequence of the French Revolution?
- What was the most significant cause of the fall of the Roman Empire?
- Which historians have made the most significant contributions to historical thought?
- What human phenomena are most important for historians to study and write about, if we are to use knowledge of these phenomena to live better in the present and future?

Historians must make many judgments while constructing historical narratives. They must determine which questions are worth asking, which sources are needed to answer the question, how to frame the inquiry so that readers appreciate and understand the significance of the inquiry, which avenues of thinking to pursue, and which to ignore.

Making judgments and interpreting history is central to historians' work. Historians routinely deal with questions that often have multiple possible answers, and with sources that frequently must be interpreted and contextualized. The answers to questions about history and the insights historians may lend to a particular problem often point the way to new considerations, rather than absolute and definitive conclusions.

Historians work with empirical data to gain a sense of the past and to construct insights about that which cannot be absolutely and precisely known. The historian knows, for example, that on July 3, 1863, approximately 12,500 Confederate troops charged Union soldiers poised at Cemetery Ridge near Gettysburg, Pennsylvania; the historian knows that the assault, led by Major General George Pickett, resulted in horrible losses for his division and that the Union claimed victory at the Battle of Gettysburg. So what is the problem? We do not immediately know, for example, the motives of men who made the decision to execute Pickett's charge despite the conditions, the degree to which the Confederate defeat at Gettysburg affected the Confederacy's will to fight, and what long-range implications the Battle of Gettysburg had on the Senators and Representatives of Pennsylvania who would one day craft the terms of Reconstruction. There are many more questions to be asked regarding the Battle of Gettysburg, but one can readily see here that the historian is not merely chasing facts to fill in a chronology; the historian is after the meaning and the significance of the events; he or she is looking for ways to explain why things happened the way they did, what subtle variables may have played a potent part in the events, and what long-lasting impact events may have had.

Different historians take different views of the same events. This often results from the "frames" through which they view the past. While most people who live in the states that fought in the Union, during the war that occupied the United States from 1861-1865, call the conflict the "Civil War," many who live in states that fought with the Confederacy refer to the conflict as the "War of Northern Aggression." The difference is important because each label contains a perspective, and perhaps even an attitude, towards the event and those who engaged in it.

Questions of judgment have often been guided by particular schools of thought that frame the authors' views of the world, events of the past, and the meaning of events in the past. As a student, before you read historical narratives and theses, it is helpful for you to know something about these schools of thought so you can begin to recognize the authors' perspective as a critical element in the text.

Distinguishing Inert Information and Activated Ignorance from Activated Knowledge in History

The mind can take in historical information in three distinctive ways: by internalizing inert information, by forming activated ignorance, and by achieving activated knowledge.

By inert information, we mean taking into the mind information that, though memorized, we do not understand. For example, many children learn in school that democracy is government of the people, by the people, for the people. But most people could not explain the difference between these three conditions. Much human information is, in the mind of the people who possess it, merely empty words (inert or dead in the mind). Much of history is learned in this way in schools. Students memorize dates and names and places, but this information is disconnected from any important ideas that concern them. Therefore, the information is of no use. It has no potency or power in the mind.

By activated ignorance, we mean taking into the mind, and actively using, information that is false. For example, the philosopher René Descartes came to confidently believe that animals have no actual feelings but are simply robotic machines. Based on this activated ignorance, he performed painful experiments on animals and interpreted their cries of pain as mere noises. Wherever activated ignorance exists, it is dangerous. When nations write historical narratives that systematically ignore the things they have done to oppress certain peoples, they are able to conceptualize themselves in glorified terms. They are able to deceive themselves into believing they are not responsible for their oppressive actions and tendencies.

By activated knowledge, we mean taking into the mind, and actively using, information that is not only true but that, when insightfully understood, leads us by implication to more and more knowledge. For example, knowledge of critical thinking skills is activated knowledge when we use these skills over and over in the acquisition of knowledge in multiple fields. Knowing that history is always told from some perspective, and that any given perspective may be based in high or low quality reasoning, is activated knowledge that helps us effectively assess differing historical perspectives.

Activated knowledge is the ultimate goal of education. When we have it, it transforms us. For example, when we truly recognize how social groups tend to exercise control over our behavior, we bring a unique perspective to every social situation. We don't simply observe human behavior. We observe conformity, manipulation, and self-deception. Or again, when we recognize that the news media's goal is not public education but profit making, we are not surprised by their lack of global perspective and emphasis on sensationalism.

We realize that putting a reader-friendly spin on every story is a way to increase readership and sales. All of these realities are illuminated through historical thinking.

Activated knowledge is a key to lifelong learning. In history, seek the knowledge that can guide your thinking to further and further knowledge. Seek foundational principles. Seek basic laws and theories. Seek fundamental ideas. Use them as guideposts in learning further ideas in history and for learning ideas in other disciplines that connect with historical thinking.

Essential Idea: There are three very different ways to take in information while learning history:
1. In a way that it is meaningless to you,
2. In a misleading way, and
3. In a way that leads you to important knowledge through which you can acquire further knowledge and insight.

Exploring Key Ideas Within History

In this section we present you with two exercises that can help you think deeply about history and historical concepts. By stating, elaborating, exemplifying, and illustrating historical ideas, you will find yourself engaged in writing history substantively.

For example, consider answering the following questions, as part of the process of learning to think historically:

- Can you state, in one simple sentence, a reasonable meaning of "the misuse of power"?
- Could you elaborate more fully what is involved in the misuse of power?
- Could you give me an example from history of the misuse of power?
- Could you give me an analogy or metaphor to help me better understand the misuse of power?

The same four questions can be formulated for explaining a democracy, a revolution, cause and effect, oppression, feminism, social norms, societal taboos, and indeed any important historical concept whatever. Every subject is a network or system of concepts that must be internalized to think successfully within it. When we can answer these four questions for fundamental concepts within history, we begin to take command of both the concepts within history and history itself.

Exercise 1
Beginning to Internalize a Key Concept in History

We can now suggest a practice pattern for beginning to internalizing any concept in history, say "x," where "x" might be, for instance, "the misuse of power in history." Here is the pattern:

1. "The misuse of power in history" might be best understood…
   (State in one or a few sentences the main idea.)

2. In other words…
   (Elaborate the idea in as many sentences as seem appropriate for the context. Consider using connectors like – "To put it another way," "To elaborate," or "To unpack this idea"…)

3. For example…
   (Give one or more real life examples from history to support the concept.)

4. To illustrate…
   (Give an analogy or metaphor from another domain of thought to help the reader understand the main concept. "The misuse of power in history" is like…)

Example of Exercise 1:
Beginning to Internalize a Key Concept in History

We will now exemplify the practice suggested above focusing on "the role of oppression" in history.

1. "The role of oppression" in history might be best understood as the tendency of people in positions of power, throughout history, to wield power over those with less power for purposes of selfish and vested interests, without regard to the rights and needs of those being oppressed. Oppression entails the unethical use of power over those with little or no choice as to their circumstances and generally involves some form of exploitation, cruelty and suffering on the part of the oppressed.

2. [In other words,] if we carefully study any historical period, we can often identify many instances of oppression, which comes in many forms. Focusing on any given set of historical events, we will find that some people will have more power than others and will often use that power in ways oppressive to those with little or no power. This is connected with the natural occurrence of stratification, which has existed throughout recorded history. Oppression is often overlooked or rationalized when those in the mainstream hold views that support authoritarian ideologies. For instance, throughout history, slavery of millions of people, often in ghastly conditions, has been countenanced by many "advanced" or "civilized" societies and cultures.

3. For examples of oppression historically, consider slavery in the Americas in the 17th through 19th centuries. Or consider the ways in which native peoples in the US were systematically lied to by the American government, removed from their lands, and driven further and further into poverty, subjugation and persecution.

    Oppression is not limited to humans acting unethically toward other humans; it is mirrored (arguably) in unethical behavior of humans in relation to "animals" over which they exercise power. For example, it is not uncommon for humans to cause unnecessary pain and suffering to higher order animals they conceptualize as just so much "stock" (livestock). Consider the act of keeping animals in boxlike cages or containers for the whole of their lives for the purposes of raising them for human consumption, in other words, keeping them in living conditions in which these animals are unable to turn around or move significantly back and forth, and are unable to engage in their other natural behaviors. People who support this practice (animal farmers and ranchers, as well as the people who eat these animals) may then (arguably) be considered "oppressors" and the tight boxed animals the "oppressed."

4. [To illustrate] Looking for general patterns of oppression historically can be compared with looking for general patterns of oppression in one's own thought and behavior. Throughout history groups have oppressed other groups. Similarly, throughout our lives, we have at times oppressed others and at other times have been oppressed. We can study oppression historically, and we can study its effects in our own lives. Both are fruitful.

Practice writing your understanding of five key concepts within history using the exercise format above. Here are some key ideas you might consider:

Fascism, Social Darwinism, philanthropy, Great Awakening, Invisible Hand of the Market, colonialism, religious fundamentalism, partisan politics, due process, genocide, human dignity, balance of power, class consciousness, social stratification, social causation, the nature of human beings, historical interpretations as value laden, the role of economics in history, the oppression of people historically.

Use relevant history books or other reference materials (e.g., textbooks, books in other disciplines) to figure out the meanings of these key concepts. But always write the meanings in your own words.

Once you have written your understanding of each concept, assess your writing by re-reading the explanation of the concept (from the relevant section in a historical text or other resource). By carefully comparing what you said (and didn't say) with the explanation in the book, you can identify strengths and weaknesses in your initial understanding of the concept.

Because every discipline contains key concepts or organizing ideas that guide everything else within the discipline, it is important to learn how to write in ways that help you internalize those concepts. Key concepts enable you to grasp the big picture of a discipline. You should master these concepts before learning subordinate concepts. In the next section we provide an example of a writing exercise that will enable you to "open up" history as a discipline. The following exercise builds on the previous one.

Exercise 2
Deepening Your Understanding of Any Key Concept in History

Use the following guidelines for deepening your understanding of important historical concepts:

1. Identify the historical concept and state the definition of the concept.
2. Describe how the concept is used in the context of the narrative.
3. State the significance of the concept to the understanding of history.
4. Give an example of the concept from real life.
5. Connect the concept to other important ideas in history.
6. Give examples for the connection between the concept and other important ideas in history.

Here is a pattern for practicing the guidelines above:

1. Concept X is defined as...
2. In this context, concept X is used in the following way(s)...
3. This concept is important to the understanding of history because...
4. An example of this concept in real life is...
5. This concept is related to these important ideas in history...
6. Some examples of the connection between this concept and other important ideas from history are...

Example of Exercise 2:
Capturing the Essence of a Historical Concept

1. The concept, Social Darwinism, is defined as the belief that there exists a natural order to humanity in which some people are endowed with greater intelligence and industriousness and that, as such, they are entitled to greater privilege and wealth.

2. In the context of this piece, "March of the Flag" (1898) is a speech by Senator Albert Beveridge; the concept is used as a justification for going to war and for American imperialism in the Caribbean and Philippine islands.

3. This concept is important to the understanding of history because it was used by many industrialized nations to expand their influence and hegemony over Asia, Africa, and Latin America. Industrial nations typically had the technological ability to impose their will on others, but rationalized this imposition with assertions that they were ultimately helping others to advance civilization.

4. An example of this might be the belief that some people currently hold, that the top 1% in the distribution of American wealth deserve such wealth (because they worked hard to get it) even if it means that many others must live in abject poverty. Another example might be the idea that students who do not express a certain aptitude or quickness in learning should not be admitted into public colleges or universities.

5. Social Darwinism is related to other ideas and concepts in history such as "White Man's Burden," eugenics, and intelligence testing.

6. Some examples of the connection between Social Darwinism and other ideas include: 1) the efforts of Lewis Terman and Robert Yerkes to develop an exam that might sort the "intelligent" from the "unintelligent" in the human population for the purposes of routing individuals to "appropriate stations" in life; 2) the sterilization laws of the United States and Great Britain at the beginning of the 20th century; 3) the Holocaust.

Conceptualizing Grade Profiles for History

In your history class, your instructor may use the following grade profiles. If so, this will help you know precisely what is expected of you in class. When your instructor explicitly fosters critical thinking within history, through understanding and routine application of the elements of thought and intellectual standards, you should become more proficient in historical thinking. You should also develop explicit intellectual tools that will help you reason better in your other classes as well as in other domains of thought.

What Each Grade Represents

The Grade of A

(The essence of A-level work. Excellence overall, no major weaknesses.) A-level work implies excellence in historical thinking and excellent performance within the history course. It also implies development of a range of historical knowledge acquired through critical thought. The work at the end of the course is, on the whole, clear, precise, and well-reasoned. In A-level work, historical terms and distinctions are used effectively. The work demonstrates a mind beginning to take charge of its own historical ideas, assumptions, inferences, and intellectual processes. The A-level student usually analyzes historical issues clearly and precisely, usually identifies historical information accurately, usually distinguishes the relevant from the irrelevant, usually recognizes key questionable historical assumptions. The student usually clarifies key historical concepts, typically uses language in keeping with educated usage, and usually identifies relevant competing points of view in history. The student shows a general tendency to reason carefully from clearly stated premises, as well as noticeable sensitivity to important historical implications and consequences. The A-level student also demonstrates an accurate understanding of historiography and the various schools of historical thought. The A-level student consistently and proficiently links causes and effects by using accurate and relevant evidence and commentary. This student readily detects contextual variables that impacted past events and easily recognizes trends, patterns, and exceptions in the human experience. A-level work displays excellent historical reasoning and problem-solving skills. The A-level student's work is consistently at a high level of intellectual excellence.

The Grade of B

(The essence of B-level work is that it demonstrates more strengths than weaknesses and is more consistent in high level performance than C-level work. It nevertheless has some distinctive weaknesses, though no major ones.) The grade of B implies sound historical thinking and sound performance within the history course. It also implies development of a range of historical knowledge acquired through critical thought, though this range is not as high as A-level work. B-level work at the end of the course

is, on the whole, clear, precise, and well-reasoned, though with occasional lapses into weak reasoning. On the whole, historical terms and distinctions are used effectively. The work demonstrates a mind beginning to take charge of its own ideas, assumptions, inferences, and intellectual processes. The student often analyzes historical issues clearly and precisely, often identifies historical information accurately, usually distinguishes the relevant from the irrelevant, often recognizes key questionable assumptions, usually clarifies key concepts effectively, and typically uses language in keeping with educated usage. The student frequently identifies relevant competing points of view within history and shows a general tendency to reason carefully from clearly stated premises, as well as noticeable sensitivity to important historical implications and consequences. The B-level student understands historiography but is sometimes inconsistent in his or her ability to identify perspectives of various schools of thought. Though the student has a sound grasp of the role of context in historical analysis, he or she sometimes overlooks subtle cause-effect relationships, trends, patterns, and exceptions in human experience. B-level work displays good historical reasoning and problem-solving skills.

The Grade of C

(The essence of C-level work is that it demonstrates more than a minimal level of skill, but it is also highly inconsistent, with as many weaknesses as strengths.) The grade of C implies mixed historical thinking and mixed performance within the history course. It also implies some development of historical knowledge acquired through critical thought. C-level work at the end of the course shows some emerging historical thinking skills, but also pronounced weaknesses. Though some historical assignments are reasonably well done, others are poorly done, or at best are mediocre. There are more than occasional lapses in historical reasoning. Though historical terms and distinctions are sometimes used effectively, they are sometimes used quite ineffectively. Only on occasion does C-level work display a mind taking charge of its own ideas, assumptions, inferences, and intellectual processes. Only occasionally does C-level work display intellectual discipline and clarity. The C-level student only occasionally analyzes historical issues clearly and precisely, identifies information accurately, distinguishes the relevant from the irrelevant, and recognizes key questionable assumptions. The student only occasionally clarifies key historical concepts effectively and uses language in keeping with educated usage. The student only occasionally identifies relevant competing points of view within history, reasons carefully from clearly stated premises, or recognizes important historical implications and consequences. Sometimes the C-level student seems to be simply going through the motions of the assignment, carrying out the form without getting into the spirit of historical thinking. The C-level student can identify elements of historiography but struggles to apply them and has difficulty detecting the schools of historical thought embodied in historical narratives. This student can see blatant cause-effect relationships, but struggles with the subtle relationships, as well as with transferring this concept

from the study of one era to that of another. Patterns, trends, and exceptions do not readily emerge in the C-level student's reading, and so history is yet conceptualized as a chronology of events. On the whole, C-level work shows only modest and inconsistent historical reasoning and problem-solving skills, and sometimes displays weak historical reasoning and problem-solving skills.

The Grade of D

(The essence of D-Level work is that it demonstrates only a minimal level of understanding and skill in history.) The grade of D implies poor historical thinking and performance within the history course. On the whole, the student tries to get through the course by means of rote recall, attempting to acquire knowledge by memorization rather than through comprehension and understanding. On the whole, the student is not developing the skills of thought and knowledge requisite to understanding history. Most assignments are poorly done. There is little evidence that the student is critically reasoning through assignments. Often, the student seems to be merely going through the motions of the assignment, carrying out the form without getting into the spirit of it. D-level work rarely shows any effort to take charge of ideas, assumptions, inferences, and intellectual processes. In general, D-level thinking lacks discipline and clarity. In D-level work, the student rarely analyzes historical issues clearly and precisely, almost never identifies historical information accurately, rarely distinguishes the relevant from the irrelevant, and rarely recognizes key questionable assumptions. The student almost never clarifies key historical concepts effectively, frequently fails to use language in keeping with educated usage, only rarely identifies relevant competing points of view, and almost never reasons carefully from clearly stated premises, or recognizes important implications and consequences. The D-level student does not understand the concept of historiography or schools of historical thought. This student tends to see events as isolated episodes which have no bearing on the present and no need for analysis as the events seem to "speak for themselves." D-level work does not show good historical reasoning and problem-solving skills and frequently displays poor historical reasoning and problem-solving skills.

The Grade of F

(The essence of F-level work is that the student demonstrates a pattern of unskilled thinking and/or fails to do the required work of the course.) The student tries to get through the course by means of rote recall, attempting to acquire knowledge by memorization rather than through comprehension and understanding. The student is not developing the skills of historical thought and the historical knowledge requisite to understanding course content. The F-level student is unable to construct accurate chronologies and to accurately identify key documents and persons of interest relevant to historical questions. Here are typical characteristics of the work of an F-level student: The student does not understand the basic nature of what it means to think historically,

and in any case does not display the thinking skills and abilities at the heart of the history course. The work at the end of the course is as vague, imprecise, and unreasoned as it was in the beginning. There is little evidence that the student is genuinely engaged in the task of taking charge of his or her historical thinking. Many assignments appear to have been done pro forma—the student simply going through the motions without really putting any significant effort into thinking his or her way through them. Consequently, the student is not analyzing historical issues clearly, not identifying historical information accurately, not accurately distinguishing the relevant from the irrelevant, not identifying key questionable assumptions. The student is not clarifying key historical concepts, not identifying relevant competing historical points of view, not reasoning carefully from clearly stated premises, or tracing historical implications and consequences. The F-level student does not understand historiography and tends to believe that while history can be interpreted, interpretations are legitimate by virtue of the individual's right to free speech and not whether they are based in critical thought. The student's work does not display discernible historical reasoning and problem-solving skills.

Part Three:
Understanding Critical Thinking
as the Key to Historical Thought

It is important to understand the essential dimensions of critical thinking and how they interface with historical thinking. In this section we introduce these dimensions and some of their connections with historical reasoning. We can begin with this overview:

Historians who think critically routinely apply *intellectual standards* to the *elements of thought* as they seek to develop intellectual virtues.

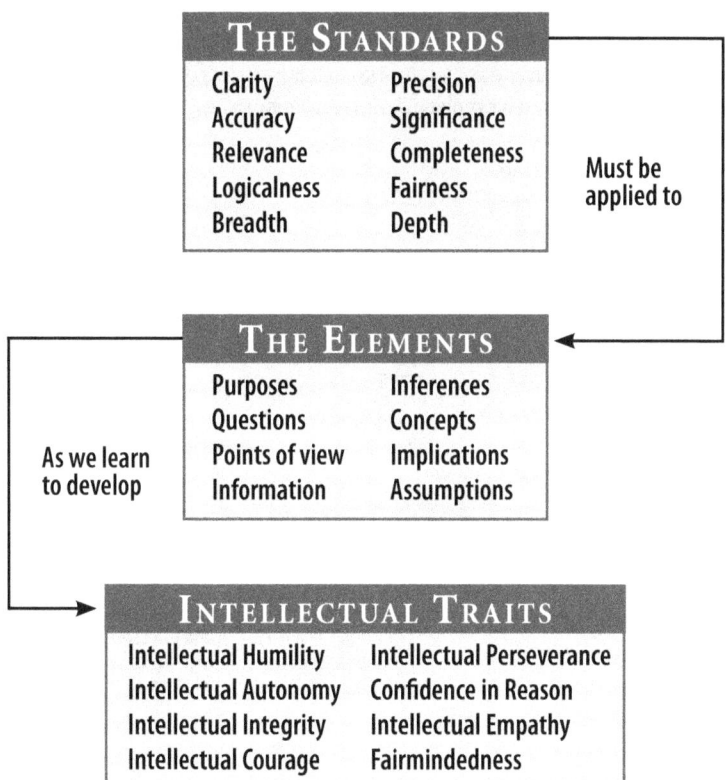

THE STANDARDS		Must be applied to
Clarity	Precision	
Accuracy	Significance	
Relevance	Completeness	
Logicalness	Fairness	
Breadth	Depth	

	THE ELEMENTS	
As we learn to develop	Purposes	Inferences
	Questions	Concepts
	Points of view	Implications
	Information	Assumptions

INTELLECTUAL TRAITS	
Intellectual Humility	Intellectual Perseverance
Intellectual Autonomy	Confidence in Reason
Intellectual Integrity	Intellectual Empathy
Intellectual Courage	Fairmindedness

Analyzing Historical Thought

To reason well about history or the topics that emerge in historical studies, it is essential to analyze historical thought by focusing on the elements of reasoning embedded in it. But first consider this argument:

> *Everyone thinks; it is our nature to do so. But much of our thinking, left to itself, is biased, distorted, partial, uninformed, or prejudiced. Yet the quality of our life and of what we produce, make, or build depends precisely on the quality of our thought. If we want to think well, we must understand at least the rudiments of thought, the most basic structures out of which all thinking is made. We must learn how to take thinking apart.*

Thinking Can Be Defined by Eight Elements

Eight basic structures are present in all thinking: Whenever we think, we think for a purpose, within a point of view, based on assumptions, leading to implications and consequences. We use concepts, ideas and theories to interpret data, facts, and experiences in order to answer questions, solve problems, and resolve issues.

Thinking, then:

- generates purposes
- raises questions
- uses information
- creates concepts
- makes inferences
- makes assumptions
- generates implications
- embodies a point of view

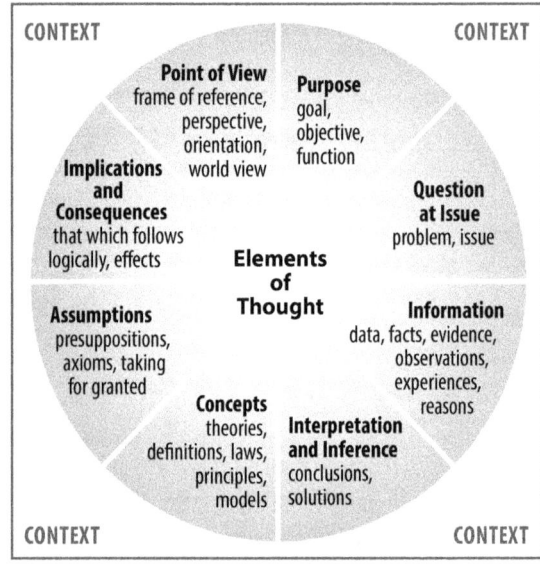

CONTEXT   CONTEXT

Point of View
frame of reference,
perspective,
orientation,
world view

Purpose
goal,
objective,
function

**Implications
and
Consequences**
that which follows
logically, effects

**Question
at Issue**
problem, issue

**Elements
of
Thought**

Assumptions
presuppositions,
axioms, taking
for granted

Information
data, facts, evidence,
observations,
experiences,
reasons

Concepts
theories,
definitions, laws,
principles,
models

**Interpretation
and Inference**
conclusions,
solutions

CONTEXT   CONTEXT

The Elements of Thought
and Questions They Imply

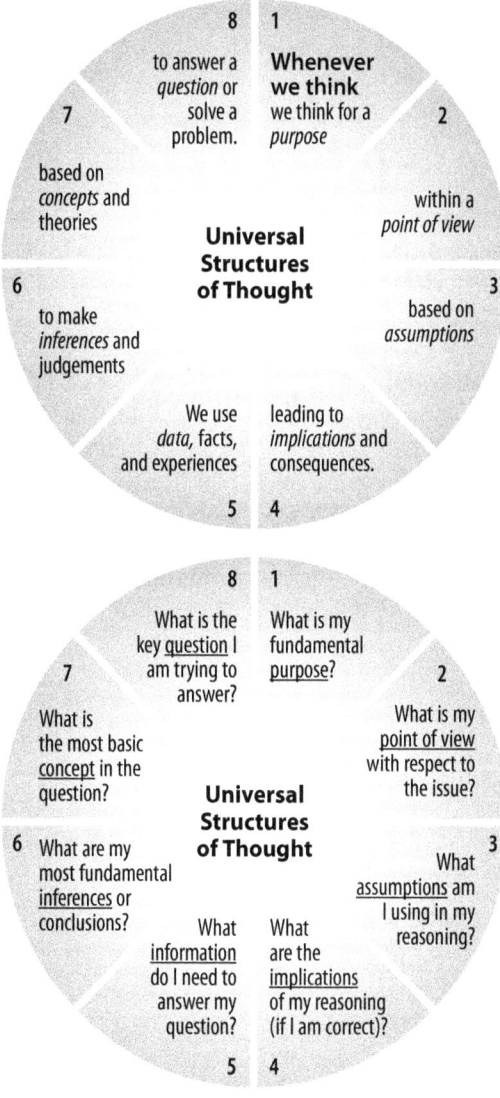

The Elements of Historical Thought

Historical Point of View
frame of reference, perspective, orientation

Purpose of Historical Reasoning
goal, objective, function

Historical Implications & Consequences
that which follows logically, results

Historical Question at Issue
problem, issue

Elements of Historical Reasoning

Historical Assumptions
presuppositions, axioms, what is taken for granted

Historical Information
data, facts, evidence, observations, experiences, reasons

Historical Concepts
theories, definitions, laws, principles, models

Historical Interpretation & Inference
conclusions, solutions

Used With Sensitivity to Universal Intellectual Standards

Clarity → Accuracy → Depth → Breadth → Significance
            Precision   ↓
            Relevance   Fairness

Essential Idea: When you understand the structures of thought, you can analyze any historical thought.

The Logic of History

The Purpose of History: To study the past in order to improve how we live in the present and the future. In studying the past, historians create narratives that are attempts to portray events as they actually occurred. When historical narratives are well constructed by historians, they can be used to improve human life.

A scholarly study of history can help us better understand complexities in issues and the merit in looking at issues from multiple perspectives. It can help us understand that change for the good often comes only in the long run. But it also helps us see that humans do not naturally progress as thinkers.

Key Questions Historians Ask: What happened during a given period of time? What caused these events to happen in this way? What were the conditions and forces that brought about these events? Are there patterns about past events that can be discovered? Do we need to rethink the way we have viewed the past in light of some new information? Have we treated as historical facts what have instead been misleading inferences or interpretations? Has some information, for the time period we are studying, been irretrievably lost? What is the most insightful interpretation of the data and information? What role does the interpretation of the "lived experience" of past peoples play in historical understanding, and how does the historian arrive at justified statements about this lived experience? Is it possible to arrive at justified interpretations of long-dead peoples, their mindsets, and their actions? How confident can we be in our statements about the past, about the features of past institutions, structures, and peoples, and about the explanatory relations among them? How does it make sense to conceptualize the events of this historical time period? What human meanings and intentions underlie a given complex series of historical events?

Key Concepts Historians Use or Have Used in Their Thinking: Historians within different specialties and with differing viewpoints use differing and often conflicting concepts in their thinking. Here are some of the key concepts historians use or have used in the past:

1. *Causation* in history, which focuses on the causes of historical events.
2. The idea of past events being depicted in the form of a narrative.
3. The extent to which there is a *grand design* in human history. In other words, whether and to what extent human history follows an inherent deterministic process (largely obsolete).
4. *The role of divine intervention* in history (largely obsolete).
5. *The role of the individual* in determining history.

6. *The role of the culture* in determining history (focusing, for instance on the extent to which cultures are oppressive to certain peoples).

7. *The role of the entire human species* in determining events.

8. The role of *class consciousness* in history.

9. The role of *social causation* in history.

10. *The role of powerful or important people* in history.

11. *The role of women* in history.

12. *The role of ethnic groups* in history.

13. *The significance* of historical events.

14. *The role of material circumstances* in human affairs.

15. *The role of economics* in human history.

16. *The role of sociocentric thought* in human history.

17. *The role of human psychology* in human history.

18. *The role of religion* in human history.

19. *Large, embracing patterns* in history.

20. *Seeking general laws* in history.

21. *Historical objectivity vs. historians interpretations as necessarily value-laden.*

22. *Historical causation* (highlighting objectivity, truth and correspondence to facts) vs. *historical narrative* (highlighting subjectivity and multiple interpretations).

Other concepts historians focus on include: Invisible hand of the market, war of attrition, collateral damage, due process, just war, balance of power, inalienable rights, representative democracy, fair wages, human dignity, fair trade, and revolution.

Key Types of Information Historians Use: Historians are generally focused on collecting, organizing, and presenting information about past events in narrative form. Information can come from, among other sources, articles, books, newspapers, magazines, scrolls, symbols, diaries, private communications between officials, letters, treaties, minutes from official proceedings, institutional reports, pictures, audio or video interviews, word of mouth, internet sources, and videos. Information may be in the form of either verifiable facts or probable facts. Often the only information available to the historian is that which has already been filtered through the interpretations of others. For instance, Socrates did not leave any written work of what has come to be known as the Socratic method. We know the thinking of Socrates only through the writings, and therefore interpretations, of others (most of which comes to us through the writings of Plato and Xenophon, both of whom were students of Socrates).

Key Inferences or Interpretations of Historians: Historical knowledge depends on procedures of empirical investigation, and the justification of historical claims depends on providing convincing demonstration of the empirical evidence that exists to support or invalidate the claim. Historians should engage in good-faith interrogation of the evidence in constructing their theories of the past. But this should not be understood to imply that there is always one uniquely true interpretation of historical processes and events. Historical interpretations are often underdetermined by the facts. Interpretations of the past will vary in accordance with the specific historical question being posed about the same body of evidence. In short, historical narratives have a substantial interpretive component, and often involve substantial construction of the past.

Some Important Implications of Historical Thinking: If historians do a good job of developing and presenting historical reasoning, and if people take historians' work seriously, the following implications may become realities:

1. People will be more likely see the importance in studying history as they will see it more relevant to their own lives.
2. People will be more likely to learn from the past.
3. People will come to recognize that all interpretations and narratives of the past are not of the same quality, and therefore they will think more critically about interpretations and narratives of the past (rather than uncritically accepting them).
4. People will be more likely to see themselves as historical thinkers and they will take greater command of the stories they tell themselves about their own past.

Some Important Assumptions That Historians Begin With in Their Thinking: Historians of different stripes will differ in the beliefs they take for granted, depending on their viewpoint, perspective and world view. But in general, here are some assumptions historians begin with:

1. That if we understand the past we can better understand humans and why they behave as they do.
2. That if we study the past, we can learn important things about people, which will help us make better decisions in the future.
3. That there is a potentially unlimited archive of information and facts that have to be sifted through and interpreted with respect to broadly-based historical questions.
4. That purported facts may not be *actual* facts, or may not be *relevant* facts.
5. That there is always the possibility that new information will become available with respect to a given historical question and when this happens, prior interpretations about historical events may need to be reconsidered.

The Points of View of Historians: The points of view from which historians look at the past will vary depending on the concepts they use in their thinking—concepts which guide their interpretations of historical information. But in general, historians look at the past as essential to understanding who we are as humans and how we can improve human societies in the present and in the future. Further, a given historian's point of view can be shaped by many potential factors: time, culture, religion, gender, colleagues, economic interest, emotional state, social role, or age group, to name a few. In addition, historians can look at the world from:

- a point in time (16th, 17th, 18th, 19th century)
- a culture (Western, Eastern, South American, Japanese, Turkish, French)
- a religion (Buddhist, Christian, Muslim, Jewish)
- a gender (male, female)
- an orientation (gay, straight)
- a profession (lawyer, teacher, …)
- another discipline (biological, chemical, geological, astronomical, sociological, philosophical, anthropological, literary, artistic, musical, dance, poetic, medical, nursing, sports)
- their own peer group, or set of colleagues
- an economic interest
- an emotional state
- an age group

Additional Thoughts on the Elements of Historical Reasoning

A reasonable approach to investigating the past entails targeting the elements of thought. For instance, it might require considering perspectives *(points of view)* of archaeologists, geologists, anthropologists, economists, biologists, engineers, political scientists, psychologists, and sociologists who play vital roles in the "re-construction" of the past.

Historical inquiry also requires that scholars apply the elements of thought in ways specific to the discipline of history. For instance, in terms of *information*, historical inquiry and reporting include primary and secondary sources of information. This information might come in the form of such artifacts as a speech, diary, letter, poem, treaty, article, film, news broadcast, or political advertisement. While all disciplines must be concerned about the source and quality of information, the historian must take special care to distinguish between primary and secondary sources, and to recognize the intentions of the originators of these sources, as well as the inherent usefulness and limitations of each. Typically, historians are concerned with the written or recorded word, and so are interested in the authorship, authenticity, credibility, and perspective of the source, the editorial processes to which the documents may have been subjected, and the function of documents at the time they were created.

These are just a few of the many ways in which historical thought is illuminated through inquiring into the elements of reasoning. Whenever historians reason about any historical issue or event, they formulate purposes, articulate questions, gather information, and make inferences based on that information. They begin with a particular historical point of view, based on their assumptions and the ways in which they conceptualize the issues. And there are implications of their historical reasoning.

Thus, it is important for both historians and instructors to be explicitly aware of, and deliberately target, the elements of thought when reasoning through historical issues, composing historical theses and narratives, and structuring historical investigations.

Essential Idea: The elements of reasoning are implicit in all historical thought. By explicitly targeting them, you can improve your ability to think historically.

A Checklist for Historical Reasoning

1.   All historical reasoning has a PURPOSE.
     * Can you state your purpose clearly?
     * What is the objective of your historical reasoning?
     * Does your reasoning stay focused on your historical goal?
     * Is your goal realistic?

2)   All historical reasoning is an attempt to figure something out, to settle
     some QUESTION, to solve some PROBLEM.
     * What historical question are you trying to answer?
     * Are there other ways to think about the question?
     * Can you divide the question into sub-questions?
     * Is this a question that has one right answer or can there be more
       than one reasonable answer?
     * Does this question require historical judgment rather than
       facts alone?

3.   All historical reasoning is based on ASSUMPTIONS.
     * What assumptions are you making? Are they justified?
     * How are your assumptions shaping your point of view?
     * Which of your assumptions might reasonably be questioned?

4.   All historical reasoning is done from some POINT OF VIEW.
     * What is your point of view? What insights is it based on? What are
       its weaknesses?
     * What other points of view should be considered in reasoning
       through this problem? What are the strengths and weaknesses of
       these viewpoints? Are you fairmindedly considering the insights
       behind these viewpoints?

Continued on page 43

5. All historical reasoning is based on DATA, INFORMATION, and EVIDENCE.
   - To what extent is your reasoning supported by relevant data?
   - Do the data suggest explanations that differ from those you have given?
   - How clear, accurate, and relevant are the data to the historical question at issue?
   - Have you gathered data sufficient to reach a valid conclusion?

6. All historical reasoning is expressed through, and shaped by, CONCEPTS and THEORIES.
   - What key concepts and theories are guiding your historical reasoning?
   - What alternative explanations might be possible, given these concepts and theories?
   - Are you clear and precise in using historical concepts and theories in your reasoning?
   - Are you distorting ideas to fit your agenda?

7. All historical reasoning contains INFERENCES or INTERPRETATIONS by which we draw CONCLUSIONS and give meaning to data.
   - To what extent do the data support your historical conclusions?
   - Are your inferences consistent with each other?
   - Are there other reasonable inferences that should be considered?

8. All historical reasoning leads somewhere, that is, has IMPLICATIONS and CONSEQUENCES.
   - What implications and consequences follow from your reasoning?
   - If we accept your line of reasoning, what implications or consequences are likely?
   - What other implications or consequences are possible or probable?

Analyzing the Logic of a Historical Article, Essay or Chapter

One important way to understand an essay, article or chapter is through the analysis of the historian's reasoning. Once you have done this, you can evaluate the historian's reasoning using intellectual standards (see pages 47-51).

Here is a template to follow:

1. The main purpose of this article is _____.
   (Here, you are trying to state, as accurately as possible, the historian's intent in writing the article. What was the author trying to accomplish?)

2. The key question that the historian is addressing is _____.
   (Your goal is to figure out the key question that was in the mind of the author when he/she wrote the article. What was the key question addressed in the article?)

3. The most important information in this article is _____.
   (You want to identify the key information the historian used, or presupposed, in the article to support his/her main arguments. Here, you are looking for facts, experiences, and/or data the author used to support his/her conclusions.)

4. The main inferences in this article are _____.
   (You want to identify the most important conclusions the historian comes to and presents in the article.)

5. The key concept(s) we need to understand in this article is (are) _____. By these concepts the historian means _____.
   (To identify these ideas, ask yourself: What are the most important ideas that you would have to know to understand the historian's line of reasoning? Then briefly elaborate what the historian means by these ideas.) See pages 35-36 for some of the key concepts historians often use in their reasoning.

6. The main assumption(s) underlying the historian's thinking is (are) _____ .
   (Ask yourself: What is the historian taking for granted [that might be questioned]? The assumptions are generalizations that the historian does not think he/she has

Continued on page 45

to defend in the context of writing the article, and they are usually unstated. This is where the historian's thinking logically begins.)

7a. If we accept this line of reasoning (completely or partially), some important implications are _____.
(What important consequences are likely to follow if people take the historian's line of reasoning seriously? Here, you are to pursue the logical implications of the author's position. You should include implications that the historian states as well as those the historian does not state.)

7b. If we fail to accept this line of reasoning, some important implications are _____.
(What important consequences are likely to follow if people ignore the historian's reasoning?)

8. The main point(s) of view presented in this article is (are) _____.
(The main question you are trying to answer here is: What is the historian looking at, and how is he/she seeing it? For example, in this thinker's guide, we are looking at "history" and seeing it as "an integrated system of understandings about the past that must be reasoned through using the tools of critical thinking.")

If you truly understand these structures as they interrelate in an article, essay, or chapter, you should be able to accurately analyze and then empathically role-play the thinking of the historian.

Essential Idea: It is possible to use the basic structures of thinking to analyze historical articles, essays, and chapters. This analysis will deepen your insight into the author's historical reasoning.

Analyzing the Logic of a History Book or Textbook

Just as you can understand a historical essay, article, or chapter by analyzing the parts of the author's reasoning, so too can you figure out the system of ideas within a history book or textbook by focusing on the parts of the author's reasoning within it.
To understand the parts of the author's reasoning, use this template:

1.   The main purpose of this history book or textbook is _____.
      (Here, you are trying to determine the author's purpose for writing the book or
      textbook. What was the author trying to accomplish?)

2.   The key question(s) that the author is addressing in the book or textbook is/are_____
      _____.
      (You are trying to figure out the key questions in the mind of the author when he/she
      wrote the book. In other words, what are the key questions which the book answers?
      Here, you might identity the most broad question the book answers, along with the
      most important sub-questions it focuses on.)

3.   The most important kinds of information in this book are _____
      _____.
      (You want to identify the types of information the author uses in the book to support
      his/her main arguments [e.g., historical documents, primary sources, historical
      interviews, etc.]).

4.   The main inferences/conclusions in this book are _____.
      (You want to identify the most important conclusions that the author comes to
      and presents in the book. Focus on this question: What are the most important
      conclusions that the author presents — conclusions that, if you understand them,
      shed important light on key beliefs in the field of history?)

5.   The key idea(s) we need to understand in this book is (are) _____
      _____. By these ideas the author means
      _____.
      (To identify these ideas, ask yourself: What are the most important ideas that you
      would have to grasp to understand the book? Then elaborate on precisely what the
      author means by these basic ideas. Begin with the most fundamental idea presented,
      such as "history, historical consequences, philosophy of history." [In a textbook, these
      can usually be found in the first chapter.] Then identify the other significant concepts
      that are deeply tied into the most fundamental one.)

Continued on page 47

6. The main assumption(s) underlying the author's thinking is (are) _____
_____.
(Ask yourself: What is the author taking for granted [that might be questioned]?
The assumptions are sometimes generalizations that the author does not think he/
she has to defend in the context of writing the book. In a textbook, the assumptions
are sometimes stated in the first chapter as the key assumptions underlying
history.)

7a. If people take the book seriously, some important implications are _____.
(What important consequences are likely to follow if readers take the book
seriously? Here, you are to follow out the logical implications of the information/
ideas in the book. You should include implications the author argues for, if
you believe them to be well-founded, but you should also include unstated
implications.)

7b. If people fail to take the textbook seriously, some important implications are
_____.
(What important consequences are likely to follow if the author's thinking
is ignored?)

8. The main point(s) of view presented in this article is (are) _____.
(The main question you are trying to answer here is: What is the author looking at,
and how is he/she seeing it? For example, the author might be looking at "history"
and seeing it as "leading to powerful insights about why humans behave as they
do.")

Essential Idea: Use the basic structures of thinking to analyze the thinking implicit in
historical books and textbooks.

The Spirit of Critical Thinking

*There is a logic to this,
and I can figure it out!*

**The logic
of historical
questions,
issues,
problems**

Essential Idea: Highly skilled historians have confidence in their ability to figure out the logic of historical issues or problems. They continually work towards logical interpretations and interrelationships among ideas. You can do the same.

Assessing Historical Thought Using Universal Intellectual Standards

The elements of thought help us analyze historical reasoning, while intellectual standards address the quality of thought. When people think historically, they often consider the source and what perspective the source represents, but they may not think deeply about an issue or set of events when they lack a broader perspective. A person who is asked, for example, to think about the impact of World War I might readily speak to how it ruined lives, killed people, destroyed farms and businesses, and cost lots of money, while at the same time neglecting its impact on the environment, the arms race, and colonialism. The purpose of adhering to intellectual standards is to improve the quality of thought and to achieve specific thresholds of excellence. There are at least hundreds of intellectual standards in ordinary languages.[A]

Universal intellectual standards must be applied to thinking whenever one is evaluating the quality of reasoning about a problem, issue, or situation. The standards are not unique to history, but are universal to all domains of thinking. To think as a highly skilled historian entails having command of these standards and regularly using them. While there are a number of universal standards, we focus here on some of the most significant.

Clarity: Understandable; the meaning can be grasped

Clarity is a gateway standard. If a statement is unclear, we cannot determine whether it is accurate or relevant. In fact, we cannot tell anything about it because we do not yet know what it is saying. Clarity is fundamental to all thinking.

Questions targeting clarity include:

- Could you elaborate further on that point?
- Could you express that point in another way?
- Could you give me an illustration or example?
- What steps might the historian take to ensure the targeted audience understands the purpose, assertions, and questions implicit in an inquiry or narrative?
- Which concepts warrant special need for explanation, exemplification or elaboration?

A   For a deeper understanding of intellectual standards, see the *Thinker's Guide to Intellectual Standards* by Linda Elder and Richard Paul, 2009. Dillon Beach, CA: Foundation for Critical Thinking Press.

Accuracy: Free from errors or distortions; true

A statement can be clear but not accurate, as in "Most creatures with a spine are over 300 pounds in weight."

Questions targeting accuracy include:

- Is that really true?
- How could we check that?
- How could we find out if that is true?
- How can we assess the credibility of sources?
- Do our sources stand up to the scholarly test of reliability and validity?
- Is this information about the past accurate? How do we know?
- What means exist to test the accuracy of reporting?

Precision: Exact to the necessary level of detail

Precision speaks to specificity. In being precise, historical thinkers provide the detail necessary for readers of their narratives to understand precisely what they are saying.

Questions targeting precision include:

- Could you give me more details?
- Could you be more specific?
- What specific questions are raised by this event or assertion?
- What details would help us understand the historical events, motives, and consequences in a more complete way?
- Have we included an appropriate amount of detail in our narrative; have we included too much detail?

Relevance: Relating to the matter at hand

Information or assertions that are relevant to an issue directly bear upon it.

Questions targeting relevance include:
- How is that connected to the question?
- How does that bear upon the issue?
- Have all relevant factors been considered?
- Has irrelevant data been included?
- Have important interrelationships been identified and studied?
- What questions about the past are relevant today and why?
- What information is relevant to a given inquiry and why?
- Does this particular representation of the past contain or omit relevant information?
- What information is relevant to our understanding the perspective of the source?
- Does this historian have a vested interest in excluding relevant information?

Depth: Containing complexities and multiple interrelationships

To think deeply is to reflect upon complexities and, where relevant, to consider subtle or hidden variables and meanings. It is possible to be clear, accurate, precise and relevant, and yet lack depth. Historical thinking usually requires one to consider multiple complexities in historical issues.

Questions targeting depth include:
- How does your analysis address the complexities in the question?
- How are you taking into account the problems in the question?
- What factors make the past difficult to understand?
- What key variables have impacted these particular events of the past?
- How do we know what motivated people to act as they did?
- Do we have enough knowledge (with sufficient sources) to create a reasonably complete picture of the past?
- Have we made a substantial inquiry into the long and short-term consequences of past events?

Breadth: Encompassing multiple viewpoints

Examining assertions and ideas from multiple perspectives enhances our understanding and is essential to historical thinking. To be broadminded is to value perspectives other than our own and to appreciate what might motivate those perspectives.

Questions targeting multiple viewpoints include:

- Do we need to consider another point of view?
- Is there another way to look at this question?
- What would this look like from the point of view of a conflicting historical theory, hypothesis, or conceptual scheme?
- Have the full range of possible interpretations been explored?
- Does the inquiry into the past identify all who were involved or affected by the events and, are their perspectives and motives adequately represented?
- Have we considered the various schools of interpretation and their contributions to the understanding of the past?
- Have we taken into account the relevant views of other social studies disciplines such as economics, geography, political science, sociology, and psychology in understanding this issue?

Logic: The parts make sense together; no contradictions

When we think, we bring a variety of thoughts together into some order. The thinking is "logical" when the conclusion follows from the supporting data or evidence. The conclusion is "illogical" when it contradicts proffered evidence, or the arguments fail to cohere.

Questions/Statements targeting logic include:

- Does this really make sense?
- Does that follow from what you said? How does that follow?
- Earlier you implied this and now you are saying that. I don't see how both can be true.
- Do the narratives we have constructed and the conclusions we have come to align with credible and sufficient evidence?
- Are the claims made about the importance of an event reasonable given the nature of events and the human condition?
- Are these historical interpretations the most logical given the available evidence?

Fairness: Justifiable; not self-serving or one-sided

Fairness gives all relevant perspectives a voice, while recognizing that not all perspectives may be equally valuable or important. Fairness in thinking seeks to acknowledge the contribution of others, respect diverse perspectives, accurately report data, and disclose potential limitations or biases.

Questions targeting fairness include:
- Have all relevant viewpoints been considered in good faith?
- Do I have a vested interest in distorting information or interpreting events in a certain way?
- Have we thought through the ethical implications of these historical events?
- To what extent do we understand the potential biases of our sources, our perspectives, and our motives in research?
- Does our narrative fairly represent important relevant perspectives and sound alternative explanations?
- Is this historian biased in dealing with this issue, and if so, why?

Significance: Important in context

Significance asks the thinker to be sure the thinking is directed towards the matters that command the greatest priority. Good historical thinking focuses on significant, rather than trivial, issues.

Questions targeting significance include:
- Is this a significant problem or issue to consider?
- Is this the central idea to focus on?
- Which of these facts are most important?
- Does the inquiry focus on matters that may significantly impact the quality of human societies?
- Does the narrative adequately speak to the importance of the issues?
- Has the historian failed to recognize or utilize important information in coming to these conclusions?

Evaluating an Historian's Reasoning

Once you understand how to analyze thinking (by targeting the elements of reasoning) and you understand the role of intellectual standards in the assessment of thought, you are in a position to evaluate any given historian's reasoning.

Here are some dimensions to consider:

1. Identify the historian's **purpose**: Is the purpose of the author well-stated or clearly implied? Is it justifiable?

2. Identify the key **question** that the written piece answers: Is the question at issue well-stated (or clearly implied)? Is it clear and unbiased? Does the expression of the question do justice to the complexity of the matter at issue?
   Are the question and purpose directly relevant to each other?

3. Identify the most important **information** presented by the historian: Does the writer cite relevant evidence, experiences, and/or information essential to the issue? Is the information accurate and directly relevant to the question at issue? Does the writer address the complexities of the issue?

4. Identify the most fundamental **concepts** at the heart of the historian's reasoning: Does the writer clarify key ideas when necessary? Are the ideas used justifiably?

5. Identify the historian's **assumptions**: Does the writer show a sensitivity to what he or she is taking for granted or assuming (insofar as those assumptions might reasonably be questioned)? Or does the writer use questionable assumptions without addressing problems inherent in those assumptions?

6. Identify the most important **inferences** or conclusions in the written piece: Do the inferences and conclusions made by the historian clearly follow from the information relevant to the issue, or does the author jump to unjustifiable conclusions? Does the historian consider alternative conclusions where the issue is complex? In other words, does the historian use a sound line of reasoning to come to logical conclusions, or can you identify flaws in the reasoning somewhere?

7. Identify the historian's **point of view**: Is the historian clear about his or her own philosophy of history? Does the historian show a sensitivity to alternative, relevant points of view or lines of reasoning? Does he or she consider and respond to objections framed from other relevant points of view?

8. Identify **implications**: Does the historian display a sensitivity to the implications and consequences of the position he or she is taking?

Essential Idea: Historical thinking can and should be evaluated by applying intellectual standards to the elements of historical thought.

Barriers to Fairminded Historical Thinking

Historians, like all of us, are subject to fallabilities intrinsic to the human mind. These fallabilities must be highlighted and dealt with at every stage of criticality. The two most significant barriers are egocentrism and sociocentrism. We cannot overemphasize the power of these two limitations in human thought. In what follows are some reminders of the nature and challenge that these represent.

The Problem of Egocentric Thinking

Egocentric thinking results from the unfortunate fact that humans do not naturally consider the rights and needs of others. They do not naturally appreciate the point of view of others nor the limitations in their own point of view. They become explicitly aware of their egocentric thinking only if trained to do so. They do not naturally recognize their egocentric assumptions, the egocentric way they use information, the egocentric way they interpret data, the source of their egocentric concepts and ideas, or the implications of their egocentric thought. They do not naturally recognize their self-serving perspective.

As humans they live with the unrealistic but confident sense that they have fundamentally figured out the way things actually are, and that they have done this objectively. They naturally believe in their intuitive perceptions—however inaccurate. Instead of using intellectual standards in thinking, they often use self-centered psychological standards to determine what to believe and what to reject. Here are the most commonly used psychological standards in human thinking:

"IT'S TRUE BECAUSE I BELIEVE IT." Innate egocentrism: I assume that what I believe is true even though I have never questioned the basis for many of my beliefs.

"IT'S TRUE BECAUSE I WANT TO BELIEVE IT." Innate wish fulfillment: I believe in, for example, accounts of behavior that put me (or the groups to which I belong) in a positive rather than a negative light even though I have not seriously considered the evidence for the more negative account. I believe what "feels good," what supports my other beliefs, what does not require me to change my thinking in any significant way, and what does not require me to admit I have been wrong.

"IT'S TRUE BECAUSE I HAVE ALWAYS BELIEVED IT." Innate self-validation: I have a strong desire to maintain beliefs that I have long held, even though I have not seriously considered the extent to which those beliefs are justified, given the evidence.

"IT'S TRUE BECAUSE IT IS IN MY SELFISH INTEREST TO BELIEVE IT." Innate selfishness: I hold fast to beliefs that justify my getting more power, money, or personal advantage even though these beliefs are not grounded in sound reasoning or evidence.

Because humans are naturally prone to assess thinking in keeping with the above criteria, it is not surprising that we, as a species, have not developed a significant interest in establishing and teaching legitimate intellectual standards. It is not surprising that our thinking is often flawed. We are truly the "self-deceived animal."

Egocentric thought plays a large role in the unfolding of historical events. Historians (and you) should take this into account when attempting to make sense of the past.

The Problem of Sociocentric Thinking

It is important for historians to understand the degree to which they have uncritically internalized the dominant prejudices of their society or culture. Sociologists and anthropologists identify this as the state of being "culture bound." This phenomenon is caused by sociocentric thinking, which includes:

- The uncritical tendency to place one's culture, nation, religion above all others.
- The uncritical tendency to select self-serving positive descriptions of ourselves and negative descriptions of those who think differently from us.
- The uncritical tendency to internalize group norms and beliefs, take on group identities, and act as we are expected to act—without the least sense that what we are doing might reasonably be questioned.
- The tendency to blindly conform to group restrictions (many of which are arbitrary or coercive).
- The failure to think beyond the traditional prejudices of one's culture.
- The failure to study and internalize the insights of other cultures (thereby improving the breadth and depth of one's thinking).
- The failure to distinguish universal ethics from relativistic cultural requirements and taboos.
- The failure to realize that mass media in every culture shapes the news from the point of view of that culture.
- The failure to think historically and anthropologically (and hence to be trapped in current ways of thinking).
- The failure to see sociocentric thinking as a significant impediment to intellectual development.

Sociocentric thinking is a hallmark of an uncritical society. It can be diminished only when replaced by cross-cultural, fairminded thinking — critical thinking in the strong sense.

When historians are unaware of the phenomenon of sociocentric thought, they are unlikely to recognize the role it plays in historical events and narratives. They will tend to uncritically assume the reasonability of a given group's ideology (because they will not be able to see through that ideology).

The Fairminded Historian

If we want to think like fairminded historians, it is not enough to develop intellectual skills and abilities. Equally important is our commitment to developing what might be called "intellectual character traits." The most important of these are: intellectual humility, intellectual courage, intellectual integrity, intellectual empathy, intellectual autonomy, intellectual perseverance, confidence in reason, and fairmindedness. The opposing traits are these: intellectual arrogance, intellectual cowardice, intellectual hypocrisy, intellectual narrowmindedness, intellectual conformity, intellectual laziness, distrust of reason, and intellectual unfairness. Let us consider each of these in order. They are crucial to the character of the fairminded historical thinker. They are antidotes to egocentric and sociocentric thinking.

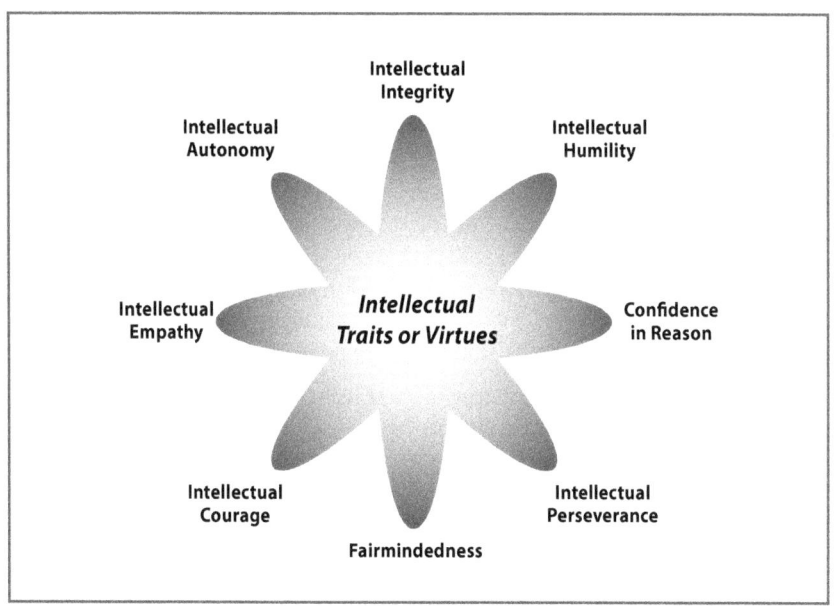

Intellectual Humility is knowledge of your own ignorance, sensitivity to what you know and what you do not know. It implies being aware of your biases, prejudices, self-deceptive tendencies, and the limitations of your viewpoint and experience.

Intellectual humility is essential to high quality historical thought. Historians are usually not eyewitnesses to the events they report and so should recognize the limits of what they can reasonably infer given their lack of first-hand information. The historian's ability to accurately represent the past is also limited by the fact that he or she cannot completely enter the minds of others to discern motives and attitudes that have shaped human decisions and actions. Again, history is not a science; it requires considerable interpretation. The historian with intellectual humility recognizes that better evidence may be forthcoming, or that people themselves may change their stories.

Questions that foster intellectual humility in historical research and composition include:

1. What do I actually know about the historical topic I am researching or writing about?
2. To what extent am I willing to consult experts on this topic; to what extent am I willing to read the works of scholars with an open mind?
3. Am I willing to seek from others critique of my historical writings?
5. To what extent do my prejudices, attitudes, or experiences influence my historical thinking?
6. To what extent do the beliefs I have uncritically accepted keep me from seeing these historical events in an unbiased way?
7. Am I open to looking at these historical events in new, more reasonable ways?
8. Am I aware of all the assumptions I have made about a given era, event, group, or person and subsequently investigated the veracity of those assumptions?

Intellectual Courage is the disposition to question beliefs about which you feel strongly. It includes questioning the beliefs of your culture and any subculture to which you belong, and a willingness to express your views even when they are unpopular.

The path to the truth may lead historians to reveal unpleasant things about national, institutional, or personal conduct. The historian has confidence that an honest account of the past, when taken seriously, can help people appreciate the complexities within and significance of most important contemporary issues and problems. Thus, intellectual courage compels the historian to make assertions and raise questions that may not be popular, but are nonetheless important and relevant. Having intellectual courage also means the historian is willing to publicly admit error when an error is committed, and has hope that redirected investigations and new inquiries will improve the accuracy, fairness, and credibility of the work.

Questions that foster intellectual courage include:

1. To what extent am I aware of the implications of my perspective and the significance of the issues I am addressing?
2. To what extent might my perspective antagonize others, and to what extent am I prepared to maintain open dialogue?
3. To what extent am I willing to adhere to reasonable beliefs which others perceive to be unreasonable?
4. Do I have the courage to give up my beliefs when sufficient evidence is presented against them?
5. To what extent am I willing to stand my ground against the majority (even though people ridicule me)?

Intellectual Empathy is awareness of the need to actively entertain views that differ from your own, especially those with which you strongly disagree. It entails accurately reconstructing the viewpoints and reasoning of your opponents and reasoning from premises, assumptions, and ideas other than your own. This trait also correlates with the willingness to remember occasions when you were wrong in the past despite an intense conviction that you were right, and with the ability to imagine your being similarly deceived in a case-at-hand.

Historians may be tempted to judge those of the past using standards of the present. Intellectual empathy entails refraining from judging the past according to today's social mores, conventions, and taboos. Further, intellectual empathy compels the historian to fairly represent the past by providing readers with a comprehensive understanding of the context in which events took place. The historian hopes to cultivate intellectual empathy in others by inviting people to deeply consider the ethical, social, political, environmental, and economic impact of human activity in a given context. The historian understands that institutional memories are often made to buttress public support for institutions and the nation that bore them (rather than present things as they are). Thus, the historian shows concern for those who may not have been well served by the vested interests of those in positions of power.

Questions that foster intellectual empathy include:

1. To what extent do I accurately represent viewpoints I disagree with in my historical writings?
2. Can I see insights in the views of those I disagree with, and prejudices in those I agree with?
3. Do I sympathize with the feelings of those people I write about who hold views that differ from my own?

4. To what extent do I understand the historical context of those who are the subject of my research and writing?

5. To what extent has my work faithfully represented the concerns, values, beliefs, and attitudes of those who are the subject of my research and writing?

Intellectual Autonomy is thinking for yourself while adhering to standards of rationality. It means thinking through issues using your own thinking rather than uncritically accepting the viewpoints, opinions, and judgments of others. It entails a commitment to analyzing and evaluating beliefs on the basis of reason and evidence, to question when it is rational to question, to believe when it is rational to believe, and to agree when it is rational to agree.

Skilled historians are mindful of the cadre of experts required to create comprehensive, fair, and accurate narratives; but they also recognize that scholarship in history is highly dependent upon the autonomous thinking that often leads to new and important insights about the past. Historians are challenged to carefully examine primary resources and evidence for themselves, and to lend their endorsement of views and assertions not based on popularity but on the merits and soundness of evidence. Historians who blindly conform to prevailing attitudes and opinions about the past risk reinforcing false claims and misinformed beliefs about institutions, groups, and individuals.

Questions that foster intellectual autonomy in historical thinking include:

1. To what extent do I tend to blindly conform to traditional historical views?

2. To what extent have I studied the primary sources on a given issue rather than relying solely on the readings of others to form my understanding of the topic?

3. To what extent am I aware of prevailing interpretations of the past and what has caused their popularity?

4. To what extent am I aware of what constitutes rational dissent in the field, and of what motivates my peers to discredit dissenting views?

5. Having thought through a historical issue from a rational perspective, am I willing to stand alone despite irrational criticism by other historians?

Intellectual Integrity consists in holding yourself to the same intellectual standards you expect others to honor (no double standards).

Consistency of thought and faithful adherence to intellectual standards are germane to the historian's scholarly work. Historians of integrity are honest about their assumptions and biases; they strive to achieve awareness of inconsistencies, omissions, and limitations of their investigations and understanding. The scholarly historian knows that the past can be interpreted in a variety of ways and thus dutifully explores credible, competing opinions to render a historical narrative as completely and truthfully as possible. At times, historians are asked to write narratives that fit neatly into the ideologies of a culture, though such narratives may not adhere to intellectual standards (but instead indoctrinate readers into unconditional loyalty and "reverence" for the nation). When historians adjust their text to suit a particular social or political agenda, their historical narratives can easily become propaganda; they display a lack of intellectual integrity.

Questions that foster intellectual integrity include:

1. To what extent are there contradictions or inconsistencies in my work?

2. To what extent does my work reflect consistency in its presentation of facts, evidence, and information to support assertions?

3. How well does my work reveal important contradictions and inconsistencies found in historical accounts, and how effectively do I account for these contradictions and inconsistencies?

4. In what ways does my work represent a well-integrated view of the past wherein the complexities of historical issues are effectively illuminated?

5. To what extent do I attempt to reduce the power of my own self-deception on my work?

Intellectual Perseverance is the disposition to work your way through intellectual complexities despite frustrations inherent in the task. It includes a sense of the need to struggle with confusion and unsettled questions over an extended period of time to achieve deeper understanding or insight.

The historian is often tasked with constructing narratives and interpretations of the past using scarce resources. In addition, the historian acknowledges that sources often have vested interests in representing their causes or experiences in a favorable light, or in representing others in an unfavorable way. Sometimes, evidence has been lost to time or deliberately destroyed, which compels the historian to approach the truth from alternative avenues. The historian knows that he or she might read volumes on a single subject and still not have all the facts. The perseverant historian retains an intense interest to learn more despite the inevitable obstacles to accessing information. Such a historian also understands that the significance and meaning of events often does not emerge until generations have passed, and so is persistent in reviewing one's own work in light of newly available information.

Questions that foster intellectual perseverance include:

1. Am I patient enough to wade through the density of sources on a given topic?

2. Do I resist the temptation to advance opinions and conclusions before I have carefully examined all the evidence?

3. To what extent have I developed a systematic approach to accessing and examining information that is difficult to obtain and comprehend?

4. Am I able to review my own work and persistently detect areas where further facts and information might yield a more accurate or logical narrative?

5. Am I willing to work my way through complexities in historical issues, or do I tend to give up when challenged?

Confidence in Reason is based on the belief that your own higher interests and those of humankind at large are best served by giving the freest play to reason. It means using standards of reasonability as the fundamental criteria by which to judge whether to accept or reject any proposition or position. It entails the belief that, with proper encouragement and cultivation, people can learn to think for themselves, to form rational viewpoints, draw reasonable conclusions, think coherently and logically, persuade each other by reason, and become reasonable persons despite the barriers to good reasoning inherent in human thought (namely egocentric and sociocentric thought).

Historians may at times be tempted to distort the truth to make a point. When this happens, such historians may imply that readers cannot be counted on to use reasoned judgment in thinking through historical issues. Further, the point of view from which the historian is reasoning may cloud her or his judgment. It is essential for historians to embody confidence in reason, to give the freest play to reason in their narratives and books. Historians should encourage people to reason through historical issues for themselves, to think through complexities in historical issues, and to decide for themselves how it makes most sense to characterize events of the past.

Questions that foster confidence in reason include:

1. Have I sufficiently clarified for myself the rationale for pursing a line of thinking, and do I have compelling evidence for my claims?

2. Do I adhere to evidence and logical assertions when persuading others of my position, or do I distort matters to support my position?

3. Do I encourage others to come to their own historical conclusions, or do I try to coerce agreement?

4. To what extent do I respect the rights of others to rationally dissent?

Fairmindedness entails being aware of the need to treat all viewpoints alike, without reference to your own feelings or interests, or the feelings or interests of your friends, community or nation. It means adhering to intellectual standards without reference to your own advantage or the advantage of your group.

The fairminded historian respects the diversity of reasonable perspectives, the concerns of all stakeholders in story-telling about the past, and the scope of logical interpretations. The fairminded historian understands the perspectives of the varied historical schools of thought. The fairminded historian is attentive to traditionally well-represented voices of the past while seeking the voices of those who have not been represented in the narrative so that the most comprehensive picture of the past might emerge. The fairminded historian understands that the selection of words used in a narrative can convey values and so takes care to articulate narratives objectively.

Questions that foster fairmindedness include:

1. Have I honestly considered all viewpoints relevant to this historical issue?

2. Am I honest about my own biases in dealing with this historical narrative?

3. Am I honest about my own biases concerning the nature of human civilization and the human condition?

4. Am I honest about my own biases concerning social rules, customs and taboos, which may affect how I deal with particular historical issues?

5. Have I adequately defined my own philosophy of history and humanity so I can readily see where my beliefs are likely to influence my research and composition?

6. To what extent am I aware of how my construction of the past may benefit or cause harm to others?

The concepts and principles implicit in fairminded critical thinking—the elements of reasoning, the intellectual standards, and the intellectual traits, understood in relationship with one another—will help you think historically in the highest sense of the term, if taken seriously. Put another way, historical thinkers concerned with fairminded critical thought routinely apply intellectual standards to the elements of thought as they seek to develop intellectual traits of mind.

These traits are the opposite of those found on p. 57.
Because these are natural dispositions of the mind, we need
to develop intellectual traits to counteract them.

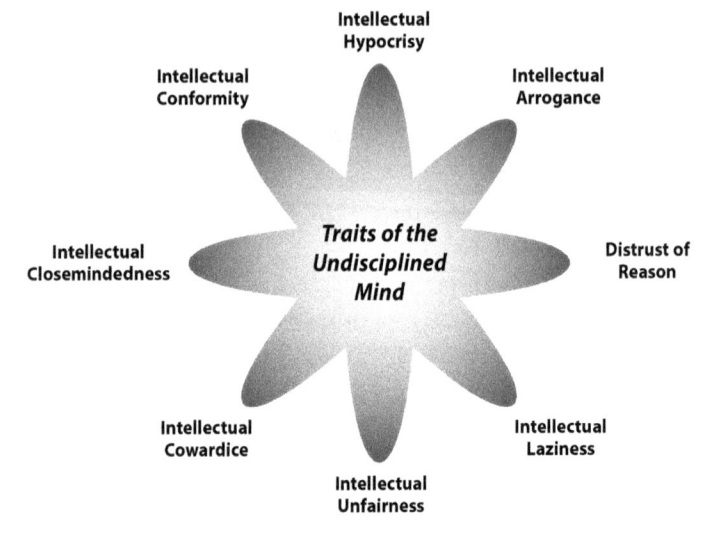

Intellectual
Hypocrisy

Intellectual
Conformity

Intellectual
Arrogance

Intellectual
Closemindedness

*Traits of the
Undisciplined
Mind*

Distrust of
Reason

Intellectual
Cowardice

Intellectual
Laziness

Intellectual
Unfairness

Essential Idea: Intellectual virtues are highly valued by skilled historians. These virtues help the historian consistently reason at a high level, and to reason fairmindedly, while thinking through historical issues.

Part Four:
Developing Further Insights into Historical Thinking

History is the long struggle of man, by exercise of his reason, to understand his environment and to act upon it.

Edward Carr, 1961

Historical thinking improves the quality of people's understanding of the past because it helps them recognize that historical narratives are constructed from available resources that may vary in their credibility and validity, that historical narratives are interpretations of the past written from the perspectives of a particular historical author, and that historical narratives often lack information because evidence is lacking or because of editorial considerations or biases. Historians who think critically in the strong sense attempt to render an understanding of the past that is thorough, evidence-based, respectful of reasonable perspectives of the past, honest about motives and consequences of human conduct, and mindful of the variables that play into the events of the past. They recognize that cause-effect relationships are not always immediate and obvious, motives are not always transparent, and evidence is not always abundant or trustworthy.

Some Challenges in Historical Thinking

Again, everyone thinks about history. We all have a personal and family history; we live in societies that ritualize the memory of certain events of the past. The ways in which we think about history, however, are often strongly influenced by others. The ways in which we think about history are affected by our egocentric and sociocentric assumptions, conceptions, and perspectives. Though schools should counter these barriers to the development of historical thought, they rarely do.

> Historians must often interpret events from the past when they can never retrieve missing information relevant to that interpretation.

History is not a linear thread from the past to the present, and it is not a science. But historians must deal with a large number and variety of scientific questions. Historians must also make scores of critical decisions to maintain the integrity of a narrative. They must determine the credibility of sources, make inferences based on evidence, interpret information and testimony, assign priority to evidence and accounts, evaluate assertions, and construct appropriate questions. They must perceive relationships between variables in order to explain correlation or cause and effect. They must evaluate the relevance of evidence and assertions, identify implications of conclusions and opinions, assess the role of social and geographic contexts in events, provide insights into motives, and interpret the significance of events, ideas, individuals, institutions, beliefs, and experiences. And they must explain what value their historical knowledge and perspective brings to contemporary conflicts and problem solving.

Since historians "reconstruct" the past by assembling existing evidence and interpreting it, the logic of history is based largely on the power of inference. We cannot physically go back in time. So we understand, by proxy, events that have occurred in the past. We attempt to construct a reasonable representation of what actually occurred. Denied the opportunity to be an eyewitness to most historical events and the privilege of knowing the subtle and hidden motives of human agents, the historian must weave a tapestry that represents a picture of the past sturdy enough to withstand the test of reasonable doubt, given the evidence. Yet, what seem to be "facts" are often merely illusion. Historians must often interpret events from the past even when missing information relevant to that interpretation can never be retrieved. And they must recognize that the information available to them (and presented as facts) may well have been fabricated or distorted in keeping with a certain view of the world. For instance, according to Carr (1961),

> *"We know a lot about what fifth-century Greece looked like to an Athenian citizen (see images 1 and 2); but hardly anything about what it looked like to a Spartan, a Corinthian, or a Theban – not to mention a Persian or a slave or other non-citizen resident in Athens. Our picture is pre-selected and predetermined for us, not so much by accident as by people who were consciously or unconsciously imbued with a particular view … The dead hand of vanished generations of historians, scribes, and chroniclers has determined beyond the possibility of appeal the pattern of the past.[8]*

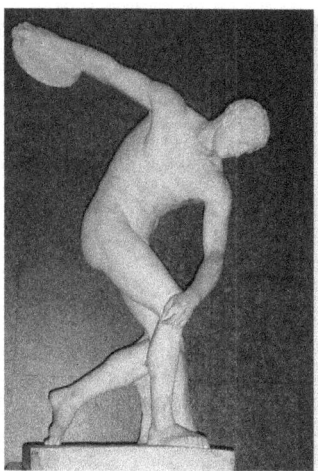

Image 1
Discobolus. Roman copy after a bronze
original of the 5th century BC.

Image 2
Statue of Roman Emperor Augustus.

These images depict how Romans are often viewed. But these pictures offer a very limited and narrow view of Roman culture and the realities implicit in the Roman Empire.

A prominent 19th century belief among historians was that history entailed collecting a maximum number of irrefutable facts. This orientation toward history is still often transmitted to students. According to Carr, this belief has lead to a

> *"... vast and growing mass of dry-as-dust factual histories, of minutely specialized monographs, of would-be historians knowing more and more about less and less, sunk without trace in an ocean of facts ... What had gone wrong was the belief in this untiring and unending accumulation of hard facts as the foundation of history, the belief that facts speak for themselves and that we cannot have too many facts, a belief at that time so unquestioning that few historians then thought it necessary—and some still think it unnecessary today—to ask themselves the question: What is history?"[9]*

Carr was concerned, not only that historians are sometimes fixated on gathering and presenting "the facts," but also that they often erroneously seek definitive ways of viewing the past. He said "any static view of history purporting to be recorded from a fixed point by a stationary observer is fallacious."[10]

It is essential to recognize that we understand history in connection with the way we see the world today, and the way we perceive the future. Carr supports this view: "... the present is an infinitesimally small moving point on a continuous line consisting of past and future. It is thus the future prospect even more than the present reality which shapes the historian's view of the past ...."[11] Carr recognized that the further back we look in history, the better we are generally able to judge issues and events. Writing in the 20th century, he says:

> *"We do not know what to think about the nineteenth century for the simple reason that the history of the twentieth century is still in the making. The historian of A.D. 2000 will be in a better case to pronounce judgment. But need we accept even his verdict – especially as it may easily be reversed by the historian of A.D. 2500?"* [12]

This problem is connected with the understanding that historians are often influenced by sociocentric thought. Most people, and most historians, do not realize the degree to which they have uncritically internalized the dominant prejudices of their society or culture. When studying history, it is important to be aware of the role that sociocentric thought might play in the thinking of any given historian.

In sum, thinking about history is often problematic because:

- Many educators, students and parents have no experience with history as a means of thinking critically about the human condition and the choices people face as consumers, citizens, and global neighbors.

- Students often don't understand that historical narratives result from editorial choices and editorial choices are subject to personal biases.

- Communities often want history lessons to inculcate a partisan view of society and encourage the individual's "loyalty" to the state rather than encouraging critical thought.

- History textbooks are often biased and frequently omit information vital to understanding the multiple perspectives relevant to historical issues.

- The structure of courses frequently prohibits in-depth exploration of how skilled historians use evidence to construct a credible portrait of the past.

- Having never been taught the requisite skills, student often lack the ability to think in complex ways about history.

- Many people in society see history as a simple tale of the past (or as dates, times and places) and therefore not as important as mathematics, science, computer technology, or other subjects associated with success in life.

> Though most educators would say that critical thinking is important to teaching history, many would not want critical thinking to lead students to conclude that "our" nation has not always been virtuous...

• People (including historians) frequently think sociocentrically about history.

As noted, history textbooks often comprise the largest source of information and exercises in a history course at the elementary and secondary levels. The content of texts, therefore, is of special concern and has found itself at the center of what some scholars and politicians have called a religious and cultural war over the soul of America's identity. A "culture war" is essentially a contest of what society should value and believe *(see image 3)*; it is a conflict over what shall be law, what shall constitute public education, what will be tolerated in the mass media, what aims shall drive foreign and domestic policies, and which perspectives will become the institutional memories of a society's history, "heroes," and "villains."[13] The vision a society embraces is frequently represented in its historical narratives (as found in history books). Visions are often rationalized by representing popular movements, policies, wars, and commercial activities as inherently virtuous even when they are injurious.

Image 3

History is sometimes viewed in religious terms as is depicted in *The sortie of Messolonghi* by Theodoros Vryzakis, 1855.

Though most people would say that critical thinking is important to learning history, many would not want critical thinking to lead students to conclude that "our" nation has not always been virtuous, or that our "heros" and leaders have acted in despicable ways.[B]

B   For an alternative text for teaching American History, see Zinn, Howard. *A People's History of the United States*. (1980; 2006). New York: HarperCollins Publishers.

The Role of Fairmindedness and Ethical Sensitivity in Historical Thinking

Voltaire's *Essay on the Manners and Spirit of Nations*, 1759, was among the first scholarly works in modern western history to recognize history as a discipline concerned with the motives and will of people, rather than the recitation of chronologies that unfolded as a matter of fate.[14] This view was radical for its time, as many scholars still regarded the course of human events as the will of God—something to be framed in theological terms that included its own measure of mystery. This very important shift in perspective laid the foundation for history as it is now perceived by mainstream historians.

> If history is to avoid being a cult of facts or a string of tales contrived to instruct its audience in social mores and customs, it must accept the challenge of critical thinking, … and refrain from irrational judgments and dualistic world views.

In directing attention to the motives and will of individuals, states, institutions, and societies, the historian assumed a new ethical obligation to be objective and broad-minded. In the early forms of history, authors were able to excuse a great deal of human malice, incompetence, vice, and weakness by laying the blame for tragedies at the feet of the gods. In this approach, there was little need to explore the complexity of cause and effect, because all was perceived as divine will. The task of probing and explaining the complexities of cause and effect requires the historian to consider the human element—the psychological forces that drive behavior, the personal virtues and vices of men and women whose actions have a wide and lasting impact, the context in which choices are cast and influenced by public opinion, the implications of technology, and the prevailing limits of knowledge.

By way of exploring and attributing motives to human beings, the historian assumed a new ethical responsibility. The historian had to be fair in assessing these matters or risk rendering a distorted or inaccurate picture of the past. This is a serious matter, as the portrayal of human motives has the power to influence the way others are judged and to affect the causes people are apt to support.

There is another ethical dimension to the historian's work, which concerns the cultivation of the reader's empathy. Historian Jacques Barzun perceived history as a guide to understanding one's neighbors rather than as a process of accumulating facts about events or documents. He penned:

> *What history teaches us is not the date of the Monroe Doctrine—that is incidental—but how such a document can come into being, why the British Navy was necessary to its effectiveness, how its meaning has changed, and*

what involvements of life and death may yet hang on it. The boy fresh from the
potato patch in Maine or Iowa may not know that he embodies the Monroe
Doctrine, but any South American is persuaded that every North American
does embody it. That is enough to affect at least two lives, for the South
American also knows to a T how he feels about the Monroe Doctrine.[15]

History can help people understand the thoughts and feelings of others and see the world and human activity from others' perspectives. It can help people empathize with others. In examining the motives, meanings, and implications of such things as a document, a speech, a law, a war, a treaty, a manifesto, an invention, or a movement, people can better understand their neighbors and improve the quality of their judgment. Without empathy, the pursuit of right and good judgment cannot be fulfilled, as it will lack understanding of what may be right or reasonable in other perspectives.

If history is to avoid being a cult of facts or a string of tales contrived to instruct its audience in social mores and customs, it must accept the challenge of critical thinking. It must respect the often-elusive evidence for one's assertions. It must refrain from irrational judgments and dualistic worldviews. Though the historian is dependent upon facts to build a narrative, and though accounts may suggest certain social preferences, the historian is largely a conductor who orchestrates a memory of the past that is rich in interpretation. And these interpretations begin with the historian's own selection of material perceived as relevant. The past is not a monolithic story that is left in the wake of previous events, but a recollection of those past events built from the memory of those who recorded their observations and those who handed down oral traditions from generation to generation. Since there are many witnesses to history, there are many testimonies; since there are many testimonies, consensus may be elusive. And every account isn't necessarily as sound as the next. Every account isn't necessarily grounded in ethical concepts and principles because people who record "history" while it is unfolding are often far from objective and are, in fact, merely recording their own viewpoint.

The historian is continuously determining which sources will figure prominently in the record and which will not; the historian must make hundreds of decisions in composing the narrative because each choice of words must convey precisely what is intended. Historians must be careful not to soil the reader's attitude with prejudice and specious innuendo. While the finished product of the historian may contain reasonable speculations based on evidence, the historian also knows there is no such thing as a finished product, for fresh evidence may emerge at any time.

Ethical historians know themselves. They are aware of their values, beliefs, assumptions, and perspectives; they are cognizant of how their idealism, realism or cynicism may impact the quality of their thinking. Ethical historians attempt continuously to detect the slightest tremor of bias in their thinking.

The ethical historian is dedicated to the discovery of and credible reporting of the past and thus considers the broadest range of perspectives and addresses the widest range of

These pictures stir the reader's imagination and remind us that all people deserve human rights even if social customs deny people those rights. Ethically sensitive historians uncover practices such as these as they study history and present their interpretations.

Image 4
Slave Trade in Early Medieval Eastern Europe.
Painting by Sergey Vasilievich Ivanov (1864-1910).

Image 5
A Persian slave in the Khanate of Kiva in the 19th century.

Image 6
"L'execution de la Punition du Fouet" ("Execution of the Punishment of the Whip") showing the public flogging of a slave in Rio de Janeiro, Brazil. From Jean Baptiste Debret, Voyage Pittoresque et Historique au Bresil (1834–1839).

interests at stake in the events. These considerations are foundational because ethics concerns the principles of goodness and justice, which by nature speak to the quality of our relationship with others.[16] The ethical historian is not afforded a myopic view of the past that takes into account only certain interests while neglecting others, for he or she understands that human actions do not emerge from a vacuum, nor are their effects quietly contained to a narrow slice of time and place.

Historians concerned with ethics do not confuse ethics with social preferences; therefore, they do not judge people and cultures based on cultural preferences. These images depict social customs that are clearly unconnected to ethics - such as preferred dress, hairstyle, and body art.

Image 7, right
A didgeridoo player in Arnhem Land, 1981, aboriginal performance.

Image 8, left
Amerikanska folk (American people), from the *Nordisk familjebok* (1904).

These two images reflect the types of raw realities that historians uncover.

Image 10, above
Street children sleeping in Mulberry Street.
Jacob Riis photo New York, United States (1890).

Image 9, below
Bodies of some of the hundreds of Vietnamese villagers killed by U.S. soldiers during the My Lai Massacre during the VietNam War.

Historians frequently encounter documentation of man's inhumanity to man, including images of terrible suffering and cruelty. The photograph on the left above, Street Children Sleeping in Mulberry Street, 1890, depicts the poverty suffered by millions in urban settings in America's Gilded Age, while the image on the right pictures civilians killed by U.S. soldiers in the Vietnam War. Historians are obliged to cover all record of mans' inhumanity to man in such a way as to stir the appropriate ethical responses to events. This means that historians must not be afraid to shock the public or the professional community by exposing images that contradict official views of the event in question. This does not make them less objective and makes their accounts more significant.

The paradox of being an ethical historian is that while he or she is concerned with how human activity has affected the broadest range of stakeholders, he or she refrains from judging and prescribing solutions to historical and/or contemporary problems based on social rules and taboos. The ethical historian maximizes his or her impact on the community by faithfully reporting events and accounting for why those events occurred, what motivated certain choices, what led some to participate and others to refrain from participation, what was known about the alternative courses of action at the time, and what consequences resulted from the activity.

It is not easy to be an ethical historian, for it requires one to imagine the world through the eyes of men and woman who have been branded as villains, traitors, and demons *(see images 11-14)*. It demands that one explore the merits of a philosophical adversary and examine the opinions of those who appear to harbor ill intentions for others. It also means that one might illuminate the view of important dissenters, or represent the voice of the poor, the vulnerable, the imprisoned and forgotten.

Nelson Mandela, once considered an outlaw by the South African Government, was imprisoned for 27 years for "subversive" and "terrorist" activities. When finally set free at the collapse of Apartheid, he served as President of South Africa. He is now considered a symbol of freedom across the world.

Image 11

Image 12

Image 13

Image 14

Image 11: Nelson Mandela circa 1937
Image 12: Nelson Mandela's prison cell on Robben Island
Image 13: Mandela in 2008
Image 14: Nelson Mandela on a 1988 USSR commemorative stamp

The historian who thinks critically and fairmindedly:

1. Presents assertions and reports of the past in reference to their original context, and calls attention to the often subtle features of that time and place to increase the reader's sensitivity to detail and accuracy.

2. Informs the audience of multiple perspectives on the matter and alternative interpretations of events, their meaning, and significance.

3. Avoids promises of easy or clear answers and solutions to complex human problems, and helps readers appreciate the fact that some matters are ambiguous and perhaps unresolvable at present.

4. Refrains from moralizing and from insisting that facts and events conform to a particular ideological world view.

5. Acknowledges that ethical dilemmas are abundant in the human experience and that the historian has the potential to help others reason through these dilemmas reasonably.

6. Is transparent about the purpose of his or her writing.

7. Avoids distorting or misrepresenting primary and secondary sources.

The ethical historian is mindful that the human being is fundamentally a storyteller and a problem-solver. Storytellers and problem-solvers want to understand why things happen as they do. When answers are not apparent or are ambiguous, storytellers and problem-solvers often invent narratives to explain the unexplainable. While there may be some facts and some metaphorical truth in the legends and myths offered as history, the historian who thinks critically is bound to separate the chaff from the wheat.[C]

Image 15

One of the many dogs Pavlov (1849-1936) used in his experiments. The saliva catch container and tube were surgically implanted in the dog's muzzle. Pavlov is "famous" for his experiments with dogs in which he studied the extent to which they salivated in connection to a sound or other stimulus. Some historians question the ethical implications of such experiments on animals.

C For a deeper understanding of ethics, see The Thinker's Guide to Understanding the Foundations of Ethical Reasoning by Richard Paul and Linda Elder, 2006, Dillon Beach: Foundation for Critical Thinking Press.

Critical Thinking and Historical Revisionism

Historian James McPherson has opined that history is under constant revision and that there is no single and absolute truth about the past and the meaning of past events.[17] History relies on eyewitness accounts that are often contradictory, documents that are frequently destroyed or not forthcoming, and the perspectives of those constructing the narrative. History must be revised when new evidence surfaces and when traditional renditions of the past are simply unable to shoulder the weight of truth.

Revisionism concerns the re-thinking and re-writing of history with fresh evidence or new perspectives. It is conducted by amateurs and professionals alike, and almost always challenges the traditional, orthodox, or official understanding of the past. Revisionism is frequently controversial. Charles Beard's *An Economic Interpretation of the Constitution of the United States* (1913) aroused the ire of his peers at Columbia and elsewhere as his thesis asserted that the authors of the Constitution created a document that represented their own material and pecuniary interests. The notion that personal profit played any part in the foundation of the Republic was, and continues to be in many circles, repugnant, as it offends the cherished belief that the Founding Fathers were motivated by philosophical and philanthropic concerns.

Revisionists act with a variety of motives and their work can be done well or poorly. One question the critical thinker must ask is, "What is the purpose of the revision?" Anti-Semites have claimed that the Holocaust never really happened; American neo-conservatives laid the blame for the Cold War squarely at the feet of the Kremlin in Moscow; and, white supremacists have blamed African Americans for their own assaults, their own lynchings, and vandalism of their own property. Historical revision conducted for the purpose of vindicating or justifying a person or group of people in the wake of false accusations and specious assertions may seem virtuous on the surface, but the real test of its merits lies in the extent to which it is true or justifiable given the evidence. The purest form of revision is that which seeks the truth (or the most reasonable interpretation) amid the tangle and debris of assumptions, opinions, political interests, distortions, lacunae, and lies; its chief objective is to render a more accurate and fair account of the past regardless of whether it upsets public authorities or is offensive to our most "trusted" institutions.

Because the long-range effects of our actions may not fully manifest themselves until one or more generations have passed, historians often revise their interpretations. The inventors of the locomotive and their contemporaries, for instance, could not have known that 80 years after the first train was set to track it would lead to the European partitioning of Africa, and that this would fuel world war and civil unrest in the 20th century; yet, this is what happened. The physicists who figured out how to split an atom could only speculate about what might happen if nuclear radiation were widely dispersed. It would be left for those who tested the bomb, and more importantly for the survivors of Hiroshima, Nagasaki, and Chernobyl, to illuminate the hideous consequences of nuclear toxicity. By virtue of enduring their consequences, every generation is a witness to the acts of their forefathers and the implications they anticipated, misunderstood, reported, or covered up.

Revisionists invigorate debate by asking difficult questions about the assumptions implicit in traditional narratives about the past, about what motivated people, and about how people were affected by the decisions of powerful individuals and the institutions they commanded. Revisionists often do their work by considering material that has routinely been ignored—the voices of women, the experiences of children, the experiences of ethnic minorities, the experiences of sentient creatures *(see image 15)*, the perspectives of the poor and vulnerable, and the world view of prisoners and those falsely accused, to name a few.

As with all historical thinking, historical revisionism should employ the tools of critical thinking. Revised versions of history are not necessarily better versions. It is important for students to become revisionists in the strong sense, using the concept of fairminded critical thinking to guide their thinking. When they do so, they are better able to look at events from the past and see them truthfully; they are better able to assess behavior from an ethical point of view and determine whether the actions of those in power have violated the people's basic rights;[D] they are better able to uncover the assumptions of those who have made important decisions and assess those assumptions for justifiability; they are better able to figure out the purposes, questions and viewpoints of people living through difficult conditions; they are better able to follow out the logical implications of historical events; they are better able to uncover the strategies people in power have used in carrying out their agendas (like political influence, manipulation, and the old boy or girl network) as against the ideas they publicly purported to believe (like justice, equality, democracy).

The assassination of John F. Kennedy, November 22, 1963, is an example of revisionist thinking in history. Traditional historical narratives report that Lee Harvey Oswald was the sole assassin of President Kennedy, yet many scholars have investigated the plausibility of a larger conspiracy. Eyewitness accounts, physical evidence, and the Zapruder film contributed to skepticism surrounding the conclusion that Oswald acted alone. In 1979, the U.S. House Select Committee on Assassinations determined that it was probable that at least two shooters were involved.

Image 17
A snapshot of Lee Harvey Oswald under arrest in Dallas, Texas.

Image 18
Some historical revisionists have argued that there was a larger conspiracy behind the murder of JFK.

D   To understand the foundations of ethics, see *The Thinker's Guide to Understanding the Foundations of Ethical Reasoning* by Richard Paul and Linda Elder, 2006, Dillon Beach: Foundation for Critical Thinking Press.

Conclusion

Historical thinking can be done well or poorly. On the one hand, all of us are historical thinkers because all of us routinely think about the past. But to what extent do we think critical about the past?

Because the skilled historian knows that institutional memories can profoundly influence events in the present and inspire people to do great harm or great good, the historian insists that history must serve but one master—truth *(see image 16)*. Though much may remain unknown about the past, what we do know must be judged in accordance with intellectual standards—standards such as accuracy, relevance, logicalness, significance, depth, breadth and fairness. Further, what we know about the past in terms of how people have treated one another and how they have treated other species, must be judged in accordance with ethical concepts and principles (such as consideration, respect, compassion, empathy, justice and integrity) rather than with ideas entrenched in social or religious ideologies, customs, rules, mores, traditions, and taboos (but which may not be based in ethics).

When historians use the tools of critical thinking as they reason historically, they think at the highest level of quality about past events, and they illuminate the past in the most insightful ways. The same is true of you. When you use the tools of critical thinking as you read historical texts and write historical papers, you are able to think deeply about the past and apply historical insights to the present and future.

Image 16

Lady Justice - Allegory of Justice - statue at a court building in the Czech Republic.

This image of Lady Justice lacks the typical blindfold and scales, replacing the latter with a book. Lady Justice symbolizes thought that is fair to all relevant parties. She reminds us that history must serve the truth. Ethical historians take into account and treat fairly all viewpoints relevant to the historical issues at the heart of their work.

End Notes

[1] Loewen, J. Lies *My Teacher Told Me: Everything Your American History Textbook Got Wrong.* (2007). NY: Touchstone.

[2] Ibid, 5.

[3] Ibid, 6.

[4] Ibid, 6

[5] Ibid, 8

[6] Ibid, 8.

[7] Zinn, H. *A People's History of the United States.* Zinn, H. (1980; 2006). NY: HarperCollins Publishers.

[8] Carr, Edward, *What is History?* (1961) NY: Random House, 12-13.

[9] Ibid, 14-15.

[10] Ibid, 13.

[11] Ibid, 12.

[12] Ibid, 13.

[13] Hunter, James Davison. (1992) *Culture wars: The struggle to define America.* New York: Basic Books.

[14] Lowith, K. *Meaning in History.* Chicago, IL: University of Chicago, 1949.

[15] Jacques Barzun, *Teacher in America* (Indianapolis, IN: Liberty Press, 1944), 154.

[16] Thillly, Frank. (1912) *Introduction to ethics.* NY: Charles Scribner's sons.

[17] McPherson, J.. Revisionist historians. *American Historical Association*, September, 2003. Accessed at: http://www.historians.org/perspectives/issues/2003/0309/0309pre1.cfm July 27, 2010.

Appendix A
Recognizing Skilled and Unskilled Reasoning

In this appendix we differentiate skilled from unskilled reasoners, focusing on each element of thought individually.

Purpose

All reasoning has a purpose.

Primary intellectual standards: (1) clarity, (2) significance, (3) achievability, (4) consistency, (5) justifiability, (6) fairness

Common problems: (1) unclear, (2) trivial, (3) unrealistic, (4) contradictory, (5) unjustifiable, (6) unfair

Principle: To reason well, you must clearly understand your purpose, and your purpose must be reasonable and fair.

Skilled Reasoners	Unskilled Reasoners	Critical Reflections
take the time to state their purpose clearly.	are often unclear about their central purpose.	Have I made the purpose of my reasoning clear? What exactly am I trying to achieve? Have I stated the purpose in several ways to clarify it?
distinguish it from related purposes.	oscillate between different, sometimes contradictory, purposes.	What different purposes do I have in mind? How do I see them as related? Am I going off in somewhat different directions? How can I reconcile these contradictory purposes?
periodically remind themselves of their purpose to determine whether they are straying from it.	lose track of their fundamental object or goal.	In writing this historical paper, do I seem to be wandering from my purpose? How do my third and fourth paragraphs relate to my central goal?
adopt realistic purposes and goals.	adopt unrealistic purposes and set unrealistic goals.	Am I trying to accomplish too much in the paper?
choose significant purposes and goals.	adopt trivial purposes and goals as if they were significant.	What is the significance of pursuing this particular historical purpose? Is there a more significant purpose I should be focused on?
choose goals and purposes consistent with other goals and purposes they have chosen.	inadvertently negate their own purposes. do not monitor their thinking for inconsistent goals.	Does one part of my paper seem to undermine what I am trying to accomplish in another part?
adjust their thinking regularly to their purpose.	do not adjust their thinking regularly to their purpose.	Do I stick to the main issue throughout the paper? Am I acting consistently in pursuit of my purpose?
choose purposes that are fair, considering the desires and rights of others equally with their own desires and rights.	choose purposes that are self-serving at the expense of others' needs and desires.	Do I have a self-serving purpose, which causes me to distort the information to fit that purpose? Am I taking into account the rights and needs of relevant others in pursuing this purpose?

Question at Issue or Central Problem

All reasoning is an attempt to figure something out, to settle some question, solve some problem.

Primary intellectual standards: (1) clarity and precision, (2) significance, (3) answerability, (4) relevance, (5) depth

Common problems: (1) unclear and imprecise, (2) insignificant, (3) not answerable, (4) irrelevant, (5) superficial

Principle: To settle a question, it must be answerable; you must be clear about it and understand what is needed to adequately answer it. A deep question requires reasoning through its complexities.

Skilled Reasoners	Unskilled Reasoners	Critical Reflections
are clear about the question they are trying to settle.	are often unclear about the question they are asking.	Am I clear about the main question at issue? Am I able to state it precisely?
can re-express a question in a variety of ways.	express questions vaguely and find questions difficult to reformulate for clarity.	Am I able to reformulate my question in several ways to recognize the complexities in it?
can break a question into sub-questions.	are unable to break down the questions they are asking.	Have I broken down the main question into sub-questions to better think through its complexities? What sub-questions are embedded in the main question?
routinely distinguish questions of different types.	confuse questions of different types; thus often respond inappropriately to questions and expect the wrong types of answers from others.	Am I confused about the type of question I am asking? For example: Am I confusing a conceptual question with a factual one? Am I confusing a question of preference with a question requiring reasoned judgment?
distinguish significant from trivial questions.	confuse trivial with important questions.	Am I focusing on superficial questions while significant questions need addressing?
distinguish relevant from irrelevant questions.	confuse irrelevant questions with relevant ones.	Are the questions I'm raising in this paper relevant to the main question at this issue?
are sensitive to the assumptions built into the questions they ask.	often ask loaded questions.	Am I phrasing the question in a loaded way? Am I taking for granted, from the outset, the correctness of my own position?
distinguish questions they can answer from questions they can't.	try to answer questions they are not in a position to answer.	Am I in a position to answer this question? What information would I need before I could answer it?

Information

All reasoning is based on data, information, evidence, experience, research.

Primary intellectual standards: (1) clear, (2) relevant, (3) important, (4) fairly gathered and reported, (5) accurate, (6) adequate, (7) consistently applied

Common problems: (1) unclear, (2) irrelevant, (3) insignficant, (4) biased, (5) inaccurate, (6) insufficient, (7) inconsistently applied

Principle: Reasoning can be only as sound as the information upon which it is based.

Skilled Reasoners	Unskilled Reasoners	Critical Reflections
assert a claim only when they have sufficient evidence to back it up.	assert claims without considering all relevant information.	Is my assertion supported by evidence? Do I have enough evidence to truly support my claim?
can articulate and evaluate the information behind their claims.	don't articulate the information they are using in their reasoning and so do not subject it to rational scrutiny.	Have I been transparent about the information I am using? What standards am I using to evaluate the information? Do I have evidence to support my claim that I haven't clearly articulated?
actively search for information *against* (not just *for*) their own position.	gather only that information that supports their own point of view.	Where is a good place to look for evidence on the opposite side? Have I looked there? Have I honestly considered information that doesn't support my position?
focus on relevant information and disregard what is irrelevant to the question at issue.	do not carefully distinguish between relevant information and irrelevant information.	Are my data relevant to the claim I'm making? Have I failed to consider relevant information?
draw conclusions only to the extent that they are supported by the evidence and sound reasoning.	make inferences that go beyond what the data support.	Does my claim go beyond the evidence I've cited? Have I overgeneralized?
present the evidence clearly and fairly.	distort the data or state it inaccurately.	Is my presentation of the pertinent information clear and coherent? Have I distorted information to (unfairly) support my position?
focus primarily on important information.	focus on trivial rather than important information.	Have I included all the important information? Can I distinguish primary from secondary information? Am I focused on the trivial rather than significant information?

Inference and Interpretation

All reasoning contains inferences from which we draw
conclusions and give meaning to data and situations.

Primary intellectual standards: (1) clarity, (2) logicality, (3) justifiability, (4) profundity, (5) reasonability, (6) consistency

Common problems: (1) unclear, (2) illogical, (3) unjustified, (4) superficial, (5) unreasonable, (6) contradictory

Principle: Reasoning can be only as sound as the inferences it makes (or the conclusions it comes to).

Skilled Reasoners	Unskilled Reasoners	Critical Reflections
are clear about the inferences they are making. clearly articulate their inferences.	are often unclear about the inferences they are making. do not clearly articulate their inferences.	Am I clear about the inferences I am making? Have I clearly articulated my conclusions?
usually make inferences that follow from the evidence or reasons presented.	often make inferences that do not follow from the evidence or reasons presented.	Do my conclusions logically follow from the evidence and reasons presented?
often make inferences that are deep rather than superficial.	often make inferences that are superficial.	Are my conclusions superficial, given the problem?
often make inferences or come to conclusions that are reasonable.	often make inferences or come to conclusions that are unreasonable.	Are my conclusions reasonable in context? Are these inferences reasonable given the available information?
make inferences or come to conclusions that are consistent with each other.	often make inferences or come to conclusions that are contradictory.	Do my conclusions in the first part of my analysis seem to contradict my conclusions at the end?
understand the assumptions that lead to their inferences.	do not seek to figure out the assumptions that lead to their inferences.	Is my inference based on a faulty assumption? How would my inference change if I were to base it on a different, more justifiable assumption?

Assumptions

All reasoning is based on assumptions
—beliefs we take for granted.

Primary intellectual standards: (1) clarity, (2) justifiability, (3) consistency

Common problems: (1) unclear, (2) unjustified, (3) contradictory

Principle: Reasoning can be only as sound as the assumptions on which it is based.

Skilled Reasoners	Unskilled Reasoners	Critical Reflections
are clear about the assumptions they make.	are often unclear about their assumptions.	Are my assumptions clear to me? Why precisely am I assuming in this situation? Do I clearly understand what my assumptions are based upon?
make assumptions that are reasonable and justifiable, given the situation and evidence.	often make unjustified or unreasonable assumptions.	Do I make assumptions about the future based on just one experience from the past? Can I really justify what I am taking for granted? Are my assumptions justifiable given the evidence?
make assumptions that are consistent with each other.	make assumptions that are contradictory.	Do the assumptions I made in the first part of my paper contradict the assumptions I am making now?
constantly seek to figure out their assumptions.	ignore their assumptions.	What assumptions am I making in this situation? Are they justifiable? Where did I get these assumptions? Do I need to rework or abandon them?

Concepts and Ideas

All reasoning is expressed through, and
shaped by, concepts and ideas.

Primary intellectual standards: (1) clarity, (2) relevance, (3) depth, (4) accuracy

Common problems: (1) unclear, (2) irrelevant, (3) superficial, (4) inaccurate

Principle: Reasoning can be only as clear, relevant, realistic and deep as the concepts that shape it.

Skilled Reasoners	Unskilled Reasoners	Critical Reflections
are aware of the key concepts and ideas they and others use.	are unaware of the key concepts and ideas they and others use.	What is the main ideas I am using in my thinking? What are the main ideas others are using?
are able to explain the basic implications of the words and phrases they use.	cannot accurately explain basic implications of their words and phrases.	Am I clear about the implications of the words I and others use? For example: Does the word *cunning* have negative implications that the word *clever* lacks?
are able to distinguish special, nonstandard uses of words from standard uses.	are not able to recognize when their use of a word or phrase departs from educated usage.	Where did I get my definition of this central concept? For example: Where did I get my definition of ethics? Is this definition warranted given educated usage of the term?
are aware of irrelevant concepts and ideas and use concepts and ideas in ways relevant to their functions.	use concepts in ways inappropriate to the subject or issue.	Am I using the concept of "statesmanship" appropriately? When I use the term, am I referring to a leader with wisdom and integrity, or am I referring merely to a person in a high political office?
think deeply about the concepts they use.	fail to think deeply about the concepts they use.	For example, the concept of oppression throughout history, as I describe it, may give an oversimplified view of the problem. Do I need to consider this concept more deeply? Do I need more examples to support my point?

Point of View

All reasoning is done from some point of view.

Primary intellectual standards:	(1) flexibility, (2) fairness, (3) clarity, (4) relevance, (5) breadth
Common problems:	(1) restricted, (2) biased, (3) unclear, (4) irrelevant, (5) narrow

Principle: To reason well, you must identify the viewpoints relevant to the issue and enter these viewpoints empathetically.

Skilled Reasoners	Unskilled Reasoners	Critical Reflections
keep in mind that people have different points of view, especially on controversial issues.	do not credit alternative reasonable viewpoints.	Have I articulated the point of view from which I am approaching this issue? Have I fully considered opposing points of view?
consistently articulate other points of view and reason from within those points of view to adequately understand them.	cannot see issues from points of view significantly different from their own; cannot reason with empathy from alien points of view.	I may have characterized my own point of view, but have I considered the most significant aspects of the problem from the point of view of relevant others?
seek other viewpoints, especially when the issue is one they believe in passionately.	can sometimes give other points of view when the issue is not emotionally charged but cannot do so for issues they feel strongly about.	Am I presenting X's point of view in an unfair manner? Am I having difficulty appreciating X's viewpoint because I am emotional about this issue?
confine their monological reasoning to problems that are clearly monological.*	confuse multilogical with monological issues; insist that there is only one frame of reference within which a given multilogical question must be decided.	Is the question here monological or multilogical? How can I tell? Am I reasoning as if only one point of view is relevant to this issue when in reality other viewpoints are relevant?
recognize when they are most likely to be prejudiced.	are unaware of their own prejudices.	Is my reasoning prejudiced or biased? Have I prejudged the issue? If so how and why?
approach problems and issues with a richness of vision and an appropriately broad world view.	reason from within inappropriately narrow or superficial perspectives and world views.	Is my approach to this question too narrow? Am I considering other viewpoints so I can adequately address the problem? Do I think broadly enough about important issues?

* Monological problems are ones for which there are definite correct and incorrect answers and definite procedures for getting those answers. In multilogical problems, there are competing schools of thought to be considered.

Implications and Consequences

All reasoning leads somewhere. It has implications
and, when acted upon, has consequences.

Primary intellectual standards: (1) significance, (2) logicality, (3) clarity, (4) completeness

Common problems: (1) unimportant, (2) unrealistic, (3) unclear, (4) incomplete

Principle: To reason well through an issue, you must think through the implications that follow from your reasoning. You must think through the consequences likely to follow from the decisions you make (before you make them).

Skilled Reasoners	Unskilled Reasoners	Critical Reflections
trace out the significant potential implications and consequences of their reasoning.	trace out few or none of the implications and consequences of holding a position or making a decision.	Did I spell out all the significant consequences of the action I am advocating? If I were to take this course of action, what other consequences might follow that I haven't considered?
clearly and precisely articulate the implications and possible consequences.	are unclear and imprecise in the possible consequences they articulate.	Have I delineated clearly and precisely the consequences likely to follow from my chosen action?
search for potentially negative as well as potentially positive consequences.	trace out only the consequences they had in mind at the beginning, either positive or negative, but usually not both.	I may have done a good job of spelling out some positive implications of the decision I am about to make, but what are some of the possible negative implications or consequences?
anticipate the likelihood of unexpected negative and positive implications.	are surprised when their decisions have unexpected consequences.	If I make this decision, what are some possible unexpected implications? What are some variables out of my control that might lead to negative consequences?

Appendix B
Analyzing Your Own Historical Narratives Using the Elements of Thought

Elements of Thought	For the Historian
Purpose	What is the purpose of the narrative I am constructing? How might this investigation be used by the general and scholarly communities? What motives underlie the inquiry? What narrative of the past am I trying to construct and what is the intended audience? What is the purpose of the primary or secondary sources I am using?
Questions	What question, problem, or issue is central to the investigation? What questions am I raising about the human experience? To what extent am I considering the complexities of the questions, events, sources, and motives of those who participated in the events of the past? Is the inquiry an elaboration of established truths, a revision, or something new? Why is the subject an important one? What is the context of the event or issue? Which variables, such as geography, politics, economics, and cultural beliefs, are essential to explore?
Information	What documents and sources are vital to this inquiry or lesson? What is the source of my information/documents/evidence? Is the source credible, reliable, and is the information valid? How have secondary sources added to existing knowledge and illuminated primary sources? What has been written or broadcast about this topic before, and how do those narratives contribute to or diminish our understanding of the past? Is there sufficient historical information to effectively address this topic? Has any significant historical information been excluded from the sources? Which evidence supports which assertions? How has mass media influenced popular understanding of the issue or event?
Inferences and Conclusions	What are my key inferences and conclusions, and why might some inferences and conclusions be more significant than others? What is the current understanding of the past, and how might the new inquiry be different from previous inquiries? What is the strength of the evidence for these inferences and conclusions? Has any information been distorted to serve a special interest? How might these inferences and conclusions impact people's understanding of the past and present? What are some important alternative inferences and conclusions, and what are the merits and limitations of those options? How do the discrete data or details of events contribute to the overarching understanding of the human condition?

Elements of Thought	For the Historian
Concepts	What themes, concepts, ideas, are central to the events or biographies I am addressing? How, if at all, have these concepts changed over time? What ideas were guiding the thinking of people during this time period? Is the inquiry clear about how these concepts help frame or illuminate the human experience and events of the past? Which concepts are difficult, yet essential to understand? Is the popular understanding of the concept different from the scholarly and what is the best way to respond to that reality?
Assumptions	What assumptions have been made about the sources, events, previous interpretations, significance of the events, motives of people involved in the events, and variables impacting the event? What generalizations have been made about the past, and what are the exceptions to those general assertions? What has been assumed about those who actually experienced the events or the consequences of those events? What assumptions have been made about why a particular account of the past is valued by others? What assumptions about people's values, motives, opinions, and knowledge are embedded in primary and secondary sources? How do I know that any of my assumptions about this historical issue or time period are justifiable? What assumptions am I making about these historical events; are these assumptions justifiable?
Implications and Consequences	What are some important implications or consequences of the narratives I create? How might my representation of historical events influence my readers? How might historical constructions affect the ability of others to understand their world and empathize with others? How might this inquiry or lesson influence people at present or in the future? If I approach this historical topic as I plan to, what implications might follow?
Points of View	What point of view do I bring to my historical interpretations? What values and concerns have influenced my interpretations? What alternative historical perspectives should I consider? What views do other schools of thought bring to the historical issue that I should consider? What point of view am I attempting to engender in the mind of the reader?

Appendix C
Analyzing & Assessing Historical Research

You can use this template to assess the quality of any historical research project or paper—that of a given historian, as well as your own historical research.

1. All historical research has a fundamental PURPOSE and goal.

    *   Research purposes and goals should be clearly stated.
    *   Related purposes should be explicitly distinguished.
    *   All segments of the research should be relevant to the purpose.
    *   All research purposes should be realistic and significant.

2. All historical research addresses a fundamental QUESTION, problem, or issue.

    *   The fundamental question at issue should be clearly and precisely stated.
    *   Related questions should be articulated and distinguished.
    *   All segments of the research should be relevant to the central question.
    *   All research questions should be realistic and significant.
    *   All research questions should define clearly stated intellectual tasks that, being fulfilled, settle the questions.

3. All historical research identifies data, INFORMATION, and evidence relevant to its fundamental question and purpose.

    *   All information used should be clear, accurate, and relevant to the fundamental question at issue.
    *   Information gathered must be sufficient to settle the question at issue.
    *   Information contrary to the main conclusions of the research should be explained.

Continued on page 92

4. All historical research contains INFERENCES or interpretations by which conclusions are drawn.

 • All conclusions should be clear, accurate, and relevant to the key question at issue.

 • Conclusions drawn should not go beyond what the data imply.

 • Conclusions should be consistent and reconcile discrepancies in the data.

 • Conclusions should explain how the key questions at issue have been settled.

5. All historical research is conducted from some POINT OF VIEW or frame of reference.

 • All points of view in the research should be identified.

 • Reasonable objections from competing points of view should be identified and fairly addressed.

6. All historical research is based on ASSUMPTIONS.

 • Clearly identify and assess major assumptions in the research.

 • Explain how the assumptions shape the research point of view.

7. All historical research is expressed through, and shaped by, CONCEPTS and ideas.

 • Assess for clarity the key concepts in the research.

 • Assess the significance of the key concepts in the research.

8. All historical research leads somewhere (i.e., have IMPLICATIONS and consequences).

 • Trace the implications and consequences that follow from the research.

 • Search for negative, as well as positive, implications.

 • Consider all significant implications and consequences.

The Thinker's Guide Library

Rowman & Littlefield is the proud distributor of the Thinker's Guide Library developed by the Foundation for Critical Thinking. Please visit www.rowman.com or call 1-800-462-640 for more information. Bulk order discounts available.

For Everyone

**The Miniature Guide to Critical Thinking
Concepts & Tools, Eighth Edition**
Paperback 9781538134948
eBook 9781538134955

The Thinker's Guide to Ethical Reasoning
Paperback 9780944583173
eBook 9781538133781

The Thinker's Guide to Fallacies
Paperback 9780944583272
eBook 9781538133774

The Art of Asking Essential Questions
Paperback 9780944583166
eBook 9781538133804

**The Thinker's Guide for Conscientious Citizens
on How to Detect Media Bias and Propaganda
in National and World News, Fourth Edition**
Paperback 9780944583203
eBook 9781538133897

The Thinker's Guide to Engineering Reasoning
Paperback 9780944583333
eBook 9781538133798

The Thinker's Guide to Analytic Thinking
Paperback 9780944583197
eBook 9781538133750

The Thinker's Guide to Socratic Questioning
Paperback 9780944583319
eBook 9781538133842

**The Nature and Functions of Critical &
Creative Thinking**
Paperback 9780944583265
eBook 9781538133958

Thinker's Guide to the Human Mind
Paperback 9780944583586
eBook 9781538133880

The Thinker's Guide to Scientific Thinking
Paperback 9780985754426
eBook 9781538133811

The Thinker's Guide to Clinical Reasoning
Paperback 9780944583425
eBook 9781538133873

For Students

The Aspiring Thinker's Guide to Critical Thinking
Paperback 9780944583418
eBook 9781538133767

The Thinker's Guide for Students on How to Study & Learn a Discipline, Second Edition
Paperback 9781632340009
eBook 9781538133835

The International Critical Thinking Reading and Writing Test, Second Edition
Paperback 9780944583326
eBook 9781538133965

The Student Guide to Historical Thinking
Paperback 9780944583463
eBook 9781538133941

How to Read a Paragraph, second edition
Paperback 9780944583494
eBook 9781538133828

How to Write a Paragraph
Paperback 9780944583227
eBook 9781538133866

For Educators

The Miniature Guide to Practical Ways for Promoting Active and Cooperative Learning, Third Edition
Paperback 9780944583135
eBook 9781538133903

A Critical Thinker's Guide to Educational Fads
Paperback 9780944583340
eBook 9781538133910

A Guide for Educators to Critical Thinking Competency Standards
Paperback 9780944583302
eBook 9781538133934

How to Improve Student Learning: 30 Practical Ideas
Paperback 9780944583555
eBook 9781538133859

The Thinker's Guide to Intellectual Standards
Paperback 9780944583395
eBook 9781538133927

www.ingramcontent.com/pod-product-compliance
Lightning Source LLC
Chambersburg PA
CBHW071342260725
30125CB00007B/99